CHHOTU

CHHOTU

A NAME, A DREAM, A STORY

ASEEM KUMAR

NU VOICE
PRESS

First published by NU VOICE PRESS 2025
An imprint of Hubhawks Pvt. Ltd
www.nuvoicepress.com

This is a work of fiction and all characters and incidents described in this book are the product of the author's imagination. Any resemblance to actual persons, living or dead, is entirely coincidental.

ISBN: 978-81-988726-3-0

Printed at Manipal Technologies Limited, Manipal
Published by: Nu Voice Press

I am devoid of lust, jealousy, hatred... I keep my eyes half closed because I don't want to see the incompleteness of humankind. However, I do have a third eye which Lord Shiva will someday inspire me to open, the day I wish to see the real world.

FOREWORD

I did not set out to write a book. I set out to remember.

To remember the countless boys I've encountered over the years—at railway stations, roadside stalls, bustling fairs, dhabas, temples, and traffic lights. Always small, always swift, always present. Always "Chhotu."

I called them that too. We all do. It's a habit we've inherited as a society…summoning a nameless boy with a word that is, in itself, a dismissal of his identity. "Chhotu" is not a name; it's a role. An instruction. A convenience.

But somewhere along the way, I started wondering: What was his real name? What did he dream of when he wasn't pouring chai or running errands? What did he want to become—if he ever had the time or safety to ask himself that question?

This book is my attempt to answer those questions.

According to recent data from UNICEF, India is home to between 1.8 and 5 million child labourers, depending on how you define "work." Independent estimates put the number even higher. These are children between the ages of 5 and 17—some barely old enough to read or write—who work in fields, factories, homes, shops, and construction sites. In cities, you'll find them at your car window selling roses or magazines. In rural areas, they're often unpaid hands on family farms. Everywhere, they are visible, yet unseen.

Studies show that working children tend to suffer not only physically but emotionally. They're more likely to experience chronic anxiety, diminished self-worth, and stunted dreams.

But the story doesn't end there.

We are living in an India where even children from the margins now have access—however fragile—to the world beyond. Through a shared smartphone, a borrowed glance at a TV screen, or a viral YouTube video, these children are being introduced to possibility. They've seen influencers, doctors, cricketers, actors, coders. They may be working in a tea stall, but they know there's a world outside it. And they're starting to dream again.

Chhotu is a collection of those dreams. Ten short stories, each told in the first person, each carrying the voice of a child we've all seen but never truly listened to. They are not meant to evoke pity. They are meant to spark recognition.

Each Chhotu in this book has a name. A family. A wound. A wild hope. Some are funny, some are philosophical. Some are angry, some quietly observant. All are real—drawn from the streets, the cities, the gullies, and from the emotional memory I carry from my own journey—from the boy I once was in Ranchi to the man I am today, building a life in boardrooms but never forgetting the pavement stories that shaped me.

This book is not an academic paper or a political argument. It is a mirror. A small one, but honest.

I hope when you look into it, you see not just them, but also something in yourself.

Because every Chhotu deserves to be seen. Every story deserves to be told.

And every name deserves to be remembered.

— Aseem Kumar

Entrepreneur | Philanthropist | Author of Chhotu

INDIA MEIN WORLD-FAMOUS

As my vision gets clear, I see and I hear too. The familiar honking and dust have certainly made me come back to reality. I see the roads bustling with people, so many people, some of them just walking endlessly it seems. Some of them are ambling from place to place, directionless. I wonder what has gotten in their heads. I see some others around—they are busy working hard at their tea stalls and juice shops. Some are pulling the rickshaws and driving auto-rickshaws. The constant beep-beep of bikes and scooty horns—I am used to that, and so is everyone else here. So many people gather around at the pani puri (tamarind water balls) stall. It makes my mouth water just to think of them. Ah! What a painful, ear-splitting noise! A random rookie just passed me by on his new superbike. Rascal! With his hair gelled back and tar-black sunglasses, and of course the tight black T-shirt, he must feel like Salman Bhai himself.

He will come back here in no time; he does that quite a few times during the day. Nobody knows who gives him the money to put petrol in his bike. Some even say he shows off his bike-riding skills around the area because of the girls' school here.

Within an hour or so, the girls will be out and that is when he will be back. That took up all my attention, alright! I don't get it! What's so good about those brown girls with their hair braided like ropes in complex patterns? I will never understand. Anyway, the woman I feel is really beautiful and like no other is undoubtedly Katrina. Man, she has a beautiful smile. What a dancer she is too! *Dhoom Machale! Dhoom Machale! Dhoom!*

I'm sweating already. The daytime hits as harsh as it gets. The scorching summer sun leads the crowd to seek shade under the peepal tree where many oldies are busy wasting their time playing poker. They come here in the morning at around 11 to make sure that their spot is not taken up by any random Majnu coming to see his Laila in the school. They stay there till sunset, playing. Some of them enjoy their hookah while they're at it.

Every now and then, in this burning hell of a place, one gets to gawk at the luxury cars passing by. They come in shining from the horizon, and when they pass by these people, it seems as though time slows down. Everybody looks at the car mesmerised and peeks inside to see who's driving. I am a culprit of doing that too! Once, I looked inside and there was a middle-aged woman on the driver's seat, wearing her glasses and a green saree. She was chewing gum and held her nose high as she realised all eyes were on her. Indeed, she was as rich as her car—*Mersdiz*—a friend of mine told me the car's name. He is such a car lover that he has pasted pictures of cars all over his wall. So many cars I never knew about! He is clearly a car fanatic. I will surely own one Mersdiz in the future. And then they will gawk at me too, like I am Rajnikanth Sir, the superstar of India.

So the missus in Mersdiz left, and I sat in the dust it left behind, as did everyone else. Everything came back to how it had been in a few seconds. As if time were running in reverse! It was amazing to see. Anyway, back again to the same old boring events. By now you must have understood where I am …

This is India, the largest democracy in the world. You will find many people, *all kinds of people,* here. Rich–poor, beautiful–ugly, educated–illiterate, kind–unkind, famous–infamous, spiritual–materialistic, you catch my drift! In this mystic land of people, an endless sea that keeps on growing and growing—oh! I heard somewhere that we are the most populated country in the world now. Wow, we really did chomp down on China like that! Whose fault is that anyway? Even China is Chinese *maal* (goods) right? We Indians are the best in the whole world! No, in the whole *brahmand* (universe)! I love my India. Salute to our heroes of the past and present.

Anyway, in this endless sea of people, there are some with big names, some with not so big names, and some unknown. I feel there should be an identity card hanging around every citizen's neck so you can know what kind of names they have. You will be surprised at the strange and bizarre names people have. They are just funny. I will tell you some of them; I have come across them in the past. I cannot even contain my laughter, you'll see—Mogli Bhai, Kircket Lal, Mirchi Singh, Dollar Kanti Lal, wait, wait, there are more—Gas Trivedi, Bidi Santosh, and yeah, Gulabi Jamuni, named after the delectable sweet of India!

Now, now, I am not making these up! *Maa kasam*! I have met these people *sach-much me* (truly). I've told you about the funny ones, I'll tell you about the boring ones now. They are very repetitive, like Rahul, Raj, Sunil, Anjali, Riya, Priya, etc. You understand, right? I've heard from an old pandit ji that each and every name holds a special meaning, which is based on the planetary positions at the time of their birth according to Vedic astrology. I was like, what does *mangal* (Mars) or *shukra* (Venus) have to do with a person born here miles away on earth? Boggles my mind. Phew!

I often wonder how far away the moon is. I don't care about the other planets—I cannot see them! But the moon, it's so serene; whenever I look at it, I am reminded of my mother's face, the most beautiful face in all existence. She used to be ill and has huge dark circles around her eyes. *Par daag toh chand me bhi hai* … (Even the moon is flawed …) So I love my mother anyway. Her hair is always oiled and shiny, just like the mystical light encircling the moon. Back then, the sweet scent of jasmine oil used to tell me that I was home indeed. My nights were all spent laughing, chattering, and sleeping in her lap.

One fair night, after I had come back exhausted, I took my refuge in my mother's lap. She lovingly fed me dal chawal with her hands and kept fanning away the naughty mosquitoes. I always used to laugh at the strange song they constantly sang—no, more like, they played the reed pipe with their loooong straw-like mouth. I felt ticklish at their sound, but it was irritating. Well, I may have called the visiting snake charmers in our neighbourhood *machhar* (mosquito) at times for that reason, and what's better is I got away with it too! They chased me of course, cursing and threatening, "*Tere upar chhod duga ye saare saanp!* (My snakes will get you!)" It was fun, for there are a few things I am scared of, and a snake is not one of them.

Oops! I got a little side-tracked again. I don't know why I have this habit. Where was I? Yes, I was telling you about my sweet mother. I once asked her how far away the moon was from our home. She gave me an ethereal smile. I swear, at that moment, when I looked at her, she looked like a deity. The moon was behind her lustrous hair, and it gave her dark-in-the-night face a halo. Like an angel, she smiled at me and said, "*Ye chaand utna hi dur hai jitna mai tujse laad karti hu* (I love you to the moon and back)."

And at that moment, I realised just how far away the moon was.

Back to our little discussion on names, shall we? I was telling you about the plethora of names we have in Hindustan. Some of those names almost seem omnipresent, and so do the attributes attached with them. Like Lord Shiva himself—*har har Mahadev*—those names and identities are everywhere, no matter where you go in India. Kashmir to Kanyakumari, Gujarat to Nagaland, you're sure to find them. As I said, they are omnipresent and always available for you, just like dear Lord Shiva himself. Just like the devotees of Shiva lovingly make offerings to the *shivling* (a sign of lord Shiva) in the same way, some have been adorned with these names.

Make no mistake, the names in itself are not mysterious. No, I am dead serious. Every single person in India knows their name and uses it to summon them too. And just like the loving God comes to the rescue of their beloved, downtrodden, grief-stricken *bhakts* (devotees) they make themselves available at your disposal—ah, patience, I see you're eager to know more! I love it when I make my listeners intrigued. It's like a movie, you know, where I am the director and you are the audience. So grab your popcorn or *chana*, which I prefer, and I will surely unpack the mystery (wink wink).

Arey! I completely forgot to tell you about the dream I was having just before waking up. *Main bhi na...* Let me tell you what happened. In the dream, I was someone else—taller, much taller than I've ever been. I could tell just by the way I was looking over people's heads. Everything looked smaller from up there, the carts, the tin roofs, even the piles of trash I usually dig through. I was in a crowd, but they were all moving in the opposite direction. I didn't care, I was walking against them, chest out, arms swinging like I had somewhere important to be. Nobody pushed me or told me to move aside. It was like I was finally taking up space. I remember looking down and seeing a little boy trying to sell balloons—maybe someone like me—and nodding at him like I understood. I was walking towards the sun—orange and bright, straight ahead. I was just about to figure out if it was rising or setting when suddenly, a loud honk cut through the air and I woke up.

To be honest, I felt a little disappointed to come back to my original body. I was like, *kya yaar!* (Ugh!) But it is what it is now. Are you getting more and more intrigued now? I know you are.

Chalo, allow me to tell you something interesting. I heard this story on the radio somewhere. It went something like this…

It was by a Chinese philosopher, what was his name? Mmm… yeah, Zhuangzi! Yes! So one day, Zhuangzi fell asleep, and in his dream, he saw that he was a beautiful butterfly, flying hither-o-thither merrily. Fluttering from one flower to another. You know how butterflies fly, right? So he was enjoying being the butterfly, just like I was enjoying being the tall man in my dream. Strange are dreams, if you think about it. Anyway, when he woke up, he again found himself to be Zhuangzi the philosopher. And here is the interesting part, you know? He was caught up in a dilemma, confusion—an existential crisis! Because he could not understand if it was him dreaming to be a butterfly or a butterfly dreaming to be him. It was like *pow!* My mind was blown away when I heard this story. What a great thinking that man had. I might have judged the Chinese too harshly, hehe. I was wondering about it for so long. You know what, there's one way to find out if the story is true. I will sleep again tonight, in my mother's lap, and try hard to become a tall man again. I will make sure that I have no other dream and only that one! Then I will tell you if the story is true or not. You will stay with me till then, right? I know you will.

"*Oye Chhotu! Idhar aana zara.* (Chhotu, come here for a sec.)"

Lo! Another bhakt calling…

What? Surprised? Yeah, my name is Chhotu. Even though my parents gave me the name Jeevan at birth, everybody keeps calling me by this moniker. Now do you understand what name I was talking about? Ah-haan! Yes, *ladeez* and *gentilmen*, my name is Chhotu, and I am as omnipresent as Lord Shiva himself—okay, maybe just right after him. You agree, don't you? See, I am always there for everyone, and I am always there for them if they call me Chhotu. I know you know exactly what I am talking about. I will even go so far as to say that they should get a temple made in my name. Nah, just kidding. I can never ever compare to our great Lord Shiva.

But you have to admit, we do have some similarities… I'll tell you, listen. See, Lord Shiva lives on Mount Kailash in extreme weather conditions. I also survive really well in every weather and every place. You tell me now, don't you see a Chhotu everywhere, all over India? Yes, that's what I am talking about.

Now, there's another similarity. Lord Shiva is free of all vice; he does not have greed; he does not have any desires for himself; he does not hate anyone; he only loves and cares for all of us. I am the same way too. I also never think about what I want—I am always there for everyone else, to take care of their needs. Whenever someone calls for me or summons me, I turn up in bare feet (Lord Shiva wears no boots either) and help them out immediately. Even though they might use an indifferent or harsh tone with me, I am always there to serve and that too without a wrinkle in my brow!

I know, I know, I cannot give blessings to anyone, but I sure make the most of my mortal abilities. And there are more similarities. Have you ever wondered why my eyes are always a little hazy—just a little—as if I am not entirely here? I look into the mirror and see the eyes of a sanyasi or yogi who does not have an ounce of attachment to this world, as if no matter what, this world has nothing, is nothing. And guess who else has eyes like that? Yes, our dearest Lord Shiva. He too is least interested in the proceedings of the world. The only difference is that he has his third eye open, and I don't.

Now, I don't know what cosmic and heavenly worlds Lord Shiva sees and enjoys with his third eye, but I wish someday I will be able to enjoy the same bliss he is overflowing with. I really wish Lord Shiva will bless me someday and open my third eye for everyone to see! I wonder if they'll call me Chhotu then…

Oh look! I got lost in my thoughts again. I am not becoming a sanyasi anytime soon, nor do I know of any mantras to chant other than *Om Namah Shivaya* and *Jai Mata Di.* No, that's not a mantra, I know. My mother needs me at home for help in her daily chores. So I cannot leave her like that just yet. And wait, there are still more similarities.

You must have seen pictures of Lord Shiva, pasted or hanging, almost everywhere you walk on the streets of India. You will find them at roadside dhabas, tailor shops, vehicle repair shops, hotels, hospitals, tea stalls, not to forget, grocery shops and at the barber's too. And who else do you find at all these places? No, not the beggars sitting outside—they are too lazy to be given any title. Yes, you guessed it right, you will find a Chhotu. Now that you know of the myriad similarities between me and Mahadev, let me tell you another. Hey, now, I might take a little pride in this one, so let me fix my non-existent collar before saying it. So, yeah, I was saying that the most amazing one is I surpass the boundaries of religion! No, seriously, no one seems bothered about my religion, caste, creed, or sect. I am accepted and summoned by all—Hindu, Muslims, Sikhs, and Christians alike. I am just Chhotu, *sabka apna, chhota sa Chhotu* (I am just Chhotu, dear to all, everyone's little Chhotu).

Now, are you starting to get why I am such a crowd-favourite? Give me a second, let me just fix my non-existent sunglasses—my friend bends his like Rajnikanth Sir, *maa kasam,* mind it! All my friends are pretty talented folks. I'll tell you about all of them later.

My mother once told me that Lord Shiva is the most powerful in all existence. She also told me that we should always respect everyone because we never know when and where Lord Shiva might come across us in a different life-form. She also taught me to be as giving and innocent as our Bholenath Himself. And who am I to not listen to my dearest mother?

Achha, tell me truthfully, are you not guilty of calling a kid Chhotu sometime in your life? I know you did. See, it's nothing to feel bad about. *Shuru shuru me* (In the beginning), I used to get angry and frustrated a lot when somebody called me Chhotu instead of my real name, but one day, when my sweet mother talked me through it, I understood that someday, I will become a big man and everyone will know my name by default.

Here, let me go and attend to the call of my bhakt for a sec. Let me look around and see where the call came from. I have the ability to be there for each one of them at the same time, you know. How? Didn't I just tell you there's a Chhotu at every *nukkad* and corner in India?

"*Bolo bhai, kyu bulaya?* (Say, brother, what's the matter?)"

"*Yaha aas pas koi cycle repair ki dukaan hai kya?* (Is there a cycle repair shop nearby?)"

"*Kya dikkat hai?* (What's the problem?)"

"*Cycle ki chain bar bar utar rahi hai.* (The chain keeps slipping.)"

"*Lao mai thik kar deta hu.* (Let me fix this.)"

The guy just gives me a weird look. I keep looking at him with my benevolent and innocent face. I may have blinked my eyes twice in question.

"*Tumhe aata hai?*(You know how to do this?)"

Now, that is a bit disrespectful. I don't understand why some people even bother to question my capabilities. Don't they know by now that a Chhotu is a know-it-all and he does it all? There is absolutely nothing that a Chhotu cannot accomplish. You want me to wash your dishes? Check. I will do them *ek dum chaka chak* (spick and span). You want me to work in your factory and lift coal, sand, and other raw materials? Check. You need to run a quick errand? Wait, I will do that for you. I will go running like the wind, no, like the lightning, with my skinny legs and do that before time. You want someone to pick up your luggage? Why fear when I'm here, dear? Fear, here, dear, get it? Maybe you just want a nice *champi*! I'll do that so well you'll feel as if you are in heaven.

If you want, I'll even sing a song for you… but nobody has asked me to do that, yet. My sister sings so well, it is unbelievable! I am just waiting for the day when she is discovered by some famous vlogger or YouTuber, and then she will become a huge star overnight. And I would be her proud brother. I hope she doesn't forget me after becoming famous. She will sing along with Shreya Ghoshal and Sunidhi Chauhan, and maybe she will win a national award too.

Oops, I got a little carried away again. I am just letting you know about my sister, in case you need a poor girl to become famous. Back to the list. You want someone to pick up the rags? I'll go from street to street collecting plastic, glass, and basically anything that can be sold. Sometimes I even find coins and rupee notes in that filth. Sometimes I even find a toy or a book with many colours and illustrations! I have taken them back home a couple of times.

One time, I was planning on washing them properly and giving them to my sister, but unexpectedly enough, my sweet-like-jalebi mother became really furious. She immediately picked those up and threw them out like a javelin thrower. I was first in awe of the strength in her arms, and then I was confused again. Why would she throw them away? I had found them like an explorer would find a hidden treasure chest. It was all precious to me, and if I wanted I could have kept them all for myself, but

I had chosen to share them with my sister. I was being an ideal brother, so why did she break my heart like that?

My mother came to me, looked into my eyes, and said, "*Agar itna hi khilono ka shuk hai toh do paise kama or unse khareed ke la.* (If you fancy toys so much, go buy them with your own money.)"

Such simple words, it made sense to me.

And since then, I understand the meaning of standing on my own two feet. I aspire to become a big man someday, and then I will tell everyone about my success story. And that's why I make and save money by doing these odd jobs.

"*Koi shaq?* (any doubts?)" I ask the man who is looking at my tiny frame and wondering if I can fix his bicycle.

"*Thik hai, karo isko thik fir.* (Alright, fix it then.)"

He leaves the bicycle in my hands and sits in the shade of the adjoining tea shop. While I am at it, he orders a cup of tea and watches me carefully.

See, it's not like I just know this stuff. I spend a lot of time going around the town, keenly watching people and their jobs. Trust me, I watch and observe each and everything. *Cheel ki nazar or Chhotu ki nazar se koi nahi bach sakta* (Nothing escapes the eyes of an eagle—or Chhotu). I love just sitting and watching. I go to the tea stall and watch piping hot tea being made and served in glasses blurry from use; I sit by a construction site and watch them work; I go to the repair shop and see how they use their hands and expertise. I even watch my mother cook food, and I know how to prepare a dish or two. I make awesome aloo paratha. My sister always loves it. I wonder if I can grow up to be a chef someday.

As I fix his cycle chain, I watch my hands turn black due to grease. I cannot go home like that—my mother will become furious! Oh! Lost in my thoughts, I fail to notice that the cycle is about to fall on my little head.

The owner, who is sipping tea peacefully, jumps from his seat and shouts, "Oh Chhotu, watch what you're doing *haan*."

"Sorry, Bhaiya, *galti se,* hehe. (sorry, brother, my bad.)"

He finishes his paper cup full of tea and throws it into the dustbin. He pays for it and makes his way towards me, navigating through the dense traffic. He skilfully manoeuvres through it and arrives with a smile on his face.

"Is it done, Chhotu?" he asks as he puts his hand on my shoulder.

"Haan, it's done. You may check."

He sits down on his cycle and pedals. He keeps pedalling and pedalling to the point that he may disappear into the horizon. With each and every pedal, he seems to grow more and more confident. I on the other hand become more and more nervous. What if he never comes back? What if he never wanted to pay me for my services? What am I supposed to do now? It has happened before too. Should I chase after him? Should I just let it go? Aaah! I should have asked him before I let him ride the bicycle. Note to self: never ever deliver before payment. Remember it, remember it, remember it. Don't forget!

I sit down on the ground with my head in my hands. I keep thinking, trying to figure how much I would have gained from this job anyway. *Zada se zada* (At most), I would have gotten ten rupees, after I negotiated with him of course. But what can be done now? I have to head back home empty-handed.

But first, I have to wash my hands. Some of these bhakts can be so ungrateful, I have to admit. Anyway, I will keep offering my services with the same enthusiasm. Let me just go and find a hand pump or tap nearby if I am lucky. Otherwise I will have to ask someone to give me some water. We have water in our neighbourhood, but there are chances that my mother will see me like this. *Chalo*, let's call it a day.

"*Oye!* Chhotu!"

"Now who the bloody hell is calling me?"

Sometimes I tend to forget that I am Jeevan and not Chhotu. Oh! To my absolute delight, I see the bicycle man coming back. With a smile on his face, he stops by me and asks, "Where were you going? I was just checking how the cycle is working. *Main thoda dur nikal gya tha.* (I went a little farther.) You were leaving without getting compensation?"

"*Badhiya hai Bhaiya, apne kaam me kabhi koi kami nahi nikal sakta.* (Awesome, brother, my work is fool-proof.)"

"*Haan, kaam toh tera solid hai.* (Yes, indeed.) *Bata kitne paise hue tere?* (How much?)"

"Whatever you wish to give me."

"*Arre*, just tell me."

"Five rupees." Shit! Whatever happened to the ten rupees you were going to ask as minimum?

"Here." The guy put a coin in my palm, and I looked at it.

"Ten rupees!"

"Yes, go and have some candies." He gave me a huge smile and put his hand on my head.

It was a new and shiny ten-rupee coin.

"*Chhotu, school nahi jaate kya?* (You don't go to school, Chhotu?)"

Wow, that sends me down a spiral altogether instantly.

See, my parents had always wanted me to study hard to make something of myself. And that's why they got me admission in a government school. They brought back school supplies and uniforms for me, which I was mighty glad to receive. I tried them on and my mother put a *Nazar battu* on my forehead. She had a great twinkle in her eyes and said, "Now look, you better study hard, otherwise I will not let you enter the house, understood?"

I nodded with a huge smile on my face. It was the first time in my life when I was feeling hopeful and excited about something.

School… It's a place with a charm of its own. It's a mysterious place with huge rooms and playgrounds. Mysterious because I had never ever seen what they looked like from inside before that day. On occasions, I was able to peep through the main gate while children made their way into the premises merrily, holding hands with their friends. It seemed magical for sure. I never thought I would be able to go to a school myself someday. I was the kid who used to watch them go in and come out of their classes; I was the kid who watched them eat ice cream at the nearby ice cream carts; I was the kid who watched them wait for their parents to arrive and take them home; I was the kid who watched them play and race each other on the streets—you catch my drift, right?

Now, did you get sad for me just now? Did you feel pity for the poor Chhotu? Wait, if the answer is no, we cannot be friends. Hehe, I was just kidding. Look, yes, I was the kid who used to watch them like a lost puppy all day, but also, I was fortunate enough to make friends with some of those children!

They were almost my age too, just a little more well-dressed. One day, when I was passing my time in between errands, gawking at them, one of the kids in a group spotted me staring at them and waved. I was taken aback! What had just happened? Did I do anything wrong? Such thoughts were flitting through my mind. But then I looked at them again and realised he was waving at me with a huge smile. I looked behind me to double check if he was waving to somebody else, but no, there was just a huge brick wall behind me.

I then figured he must need some help or something from me. Anyway, I mustered up some courage to walk up to him—mind you, I was very conscious of my appearance at that moment. I quickly fixed my hair and walked up to him confidently.

"*Haan, bhai?* (Yes, brother?)"

He kept looking at me with a diamond-like smile and said, "I see you have been watching us."

Now, everyone in the group had their eyes on me. Great, I was the centre of attention. Was it good? Was it bad? I honestly don't know. I just remember being extremely self-conscious.

They all kept looking at me, and I said, "No, I was watching almost everyone here."

My mother always taught me not to lie. But at that moment I did. I don't know why?! I wasn't thinking, actually. Okay, it gives me an embarrassing feeling even to recollect it.

The kid seemed smart; he must have been the topper in his class. He said, "Look, I know you watch us every single day."

Now I had no words to say. I was speechless. What did this kid want from me? I was looking, so what? I couldn't even look now? Was I not an independent citizen of Hindustan? Thankfully enough, my silence was interrupted by his cheerful voice, "Come and play with us."

I was shocked to my bones! He was asking me to play with him. Whoa! I had seen these kids play with their expensive cricket bats and balls in the nearby field. I looked at the other kids in the group, and they immediately said, "Yes, come and play with us. We need a player today."

I was delighted, blissfully delighted. I nodded smilingly until my head was about to fall off from my body. They laughed and then I accompanied them to the field. That day, I played with them till late in the evening. It was one of the best days of my life. *Sach me*, I played to my heart's content. I laughed, I ran, and I fell down at times too. After my team won, I celebrated with all of them.

It was too late in the evening. The sun had gone down and the streetlights were on. I bid my newly-made friends goodbye for the day and left for home. My legs were hurting like hell, I remember. I was just relieved to reach home. But as soon as I set one foot on the threshold, I saw none other than Maa Kali herself, standing before me with a rolling pin in hand. I instantly fell to the ground and bowed at her feet.

"Mother, I know, I was late today," I pleaded as I kept my head down and my hands folded, begging for her mercy. *But vo maa hai na,* she does as she pleases (She's a mom, they do as they please).

She grabbed my ear and pulled me up. Ouch! I think I have a slightly disfigured ear for this reason. Thanks to Lord Shiva, my face isn't disfigured as well from all the slaps. It could be a real problem at the time of marriage, hehe.

Anyway, I kept saying sorry to her, pleading and begging for her mercy. She was so furious that her eyeballs were about to pop out. God, what a terrifying sight! She said, her voice echoing, "How dare you stay out late and never even think of informing your mother!"

"I'm sorry, Maa. Please *maan jao na* (Please forgive me)."

She pulled my ear one more time. All the joy of the whole day's play was forgotten, and all I knew was her fierce eyes. She cooled down eventually though, after I flattered her a little: "*Pyari maa, maaf kar do na. Galti se late ho gaya. Mujhe pata hi nahi chala. Aap toh sabse achhi maa ho, please gussa mat karo* (Dearest Maa, I'm so sorry. I didn't mean to be late, it just happened. I lost track of time. You're the best mother in the world, please don't be angry)." It worked, as she immediately left my ear and said, "Alright, come inside and have your dinner. I made your favourite aloo gobi sabzi today. I even asked your father to bring rasgullas. He will be here any minute now. We will have dinner together. Off you go now, wash your feet and hands."

I was relieved to see that Kali Maa was now just my Maa again. That night, while enjoying my dinner, I told my family how much fun I had playing with my newly-made friends…

That's how I even got myself wondering about school. I remember thinking to myself, *kaash mai bhi school jata* (how I wish I also went to school). That way we would all stay together and have fun.

That dream partially came true when my parents got me admission in the government school. I wonder if the reason was that I was spending too much time playing with my new friends, or maybe it was their dream for me to become one of them, or at least like them in some way.

Alright, fast forward to my first day at school. I was walking inside the gate with my backpack and a water bottle. My mother had told me that I would be served lunch in school itself. It was called the mid-day meal. I was like, cool, even my friends from the private school don't have mid-day meals. *Chalo, let's try that, too*, I thought.

My first day at school was fine, except I just found it really hard to stay put in my seat all day. It used to hurt my bottom so much! I would keep twisting and turning, my legs would feel like running away—as though they had minds of their own, and my feet would almost melt inside my leather shoes. The buttons on my shirt made me feel as if I were getting cooked—it was claustrophobic! And as if that wasn't enough, the subjects they taught us were boring too! I kept looking at the clock and desperately waited for the day to end.

My idea of school was that I would get to learn about money there, as it is the single most important thing in life after Lord Shiva himself. But they taught us nothing about how to make money. I was disappointed. But at least the mid-day meal was great, to save the day.

So when I came back home, my mother asked me how my first day at school was. I told her straight away, "Mmm, I could get used to it," in full hero *ishtyle*. She was over the moon to hear me say that. And it was true to an extent too. I really found school not so bad at all. It was my dream, after all, to be at one.

No more were my afternoons filled with roaming around and watching other school kids; it was my turn to study and become a top student. I would wake up early in the morning and polish my new shoes and make sure that they stayed as new forever. It was an absolute delight to wake up early, brush my teeth properly, and comb my hair well and make them really shiny using my mother's jasmine oil. I put on my shirt; truly, it was so white. My eyes sparkled. My mother would always feed me dahi-shakkar for good luck before seeing me off. It was a blissful routine, and an exciting one too.

There was something so intoxicating about the moment I stepped out of my house and walked onto the streets. All my neighbours would look at me as if I were a star. I would pay them no attention, and with a *chhappan inch ka seena* (chest puffed out with pride), I would keep on walking. Hehe, the neighbours gawked at me the way I was gawking at the Mersdiz that day. My hair gleamed in the rising sun, and I put my feet carefully on the ground to prevent them from getting dirty in the filth. One time, a jealous neighbour tried to ruin my uniform by riding his bike in a puddle. I was as quick as Murugan and dodged him like Bruce Lee. Then I looked at him and pointed my finger at him in pride and warning.

Once, as I walked to my school, I suddenly came across a little roadside temple of Lord Hanuman. I immediately bowed down at his feet and prayed to him to always keep my mother happy. With his blessings, I would go to school every day.

Dheere, dheere (As time passed), I was beginning to stay put in my classes. I began sitting comfortably at my desk, even liking it! I did not feel like removing my shoes anymore. And guess what? Over time, I began to like the subjects too. *Samajh aa rha tha sab finally* (It all finally made sense). And even better than that, my English teacher was a lovely lady. She was an angel, I swear. Every time she looked at me, I floated in the air with her—full Bollywood-style! I swear, she was a very pleasant presence.

So that was my life for about a month. You want to know what happened after that? Stay tuned for more! *Ase hi bolte hain na TV pe?* (That's how they do it in the TV shows, am I right?)

Okay, I'll tell you what happened. *Apne jo bapu hai na, wo construction me kaam karte hai. Vha pe diware banane ka kaam vo karte hai* (My dad works in construction, he builds walls there). One fateful day, while working on the third floor of a building, he was carrying a heavy basket full with bricks. At some point while going up the stairs, he slipped and tumbled down. As he fell, the basket of bricks flew out of his hands, scattering across the staircase. The loud crash echoed through the building, catching the attention of nearby co-workers who rushed to his aid.

He was hurt pretty badly. An ambulance was called immediately, and he was rushed to the hospital. People were just grateful that he was alive at least. He could have died on the spot. There were bruises all over his body due to the bricks that had hit him. We were aware that these kind of things were very common with construction workers. And my father was just a labourer. He worked hard all day and had been doing that for a very long time.

Despite the risks involved, my father took pride in his work and never complained. He wasn't the type to speak much. Whenever he came back home, he never said anything. He would quietly have his dinner, leave for bed, and fall asleep immediately. His dedication and perseverance were evident in the way he pushed through each day, providing for our family. We were aware of the sacrifices he made to support us. And it was his wish for me to go to school and make something of myself.

Over the years, however, his body had become increasingly weak, and he looked like a shadow of what he used to be. My mother came running to my school one day and asked for me.

I was surprised to see her there and said, "*Maa, yaha lunch banta hai boht achha, tum kyu layi?* (Mom, we have lunch here, why did you bother?)"

She was sweating all over and her breath was short. She huffed and said, wiping away the sweat from her face, "Your father, he is unconscious."

I dropped my bag where I was standing and ran to where my father was. Little did I know that it was the last time I would be seeing that bag—no, the school itself, too.

My father had worry etched all over his face. He could not move one muscle in his face, the doctor told us. He just stared at the nothingness of the wall. I could not believe how someone could live without blinking their eyes.

I stayed there by his side, watching his face for hours, waiting for him to blink or for his face to turn towards me. Oh, but wait was all I did. He never blinked, he never smiled. His expression remained frozen in time, a very long time it seemed, devoid of any signs of life or emotion. It was as if time stood still for him; he was trapped in an unresponsive state. I tried talking to him too. I cracked jokes, acted totally crazy, and even danced too. It was just me though—anybody looking from outside would feel I had gone crazy, dancing by the bed of my sick father.

The silence in his eyes was deafening, and I couldn't help but wonder if he would ever regain consciousness.

And since then, my father has been lying unconscious. He has gone into a coma, and mother toils day and night looking after him. As he was the sole breadwinner of the family, my neighbours said that I should start working as soon as possible.

And so I did. The neighbours seem to be enjoying the fact that I won't be able to go to school anymore. I want to, but how? My father would've never wanted me to leave school.

"Chhotu, I am sorry to hear this. But no matter what, you must keep on studying. You must go to school. You will get a head start in life," the guy remarks, still sitting on his bicycle.

I look up at the guy with hopeful eyes, my strong will shining through every bone in my body. "I promise, Bhaiya. I won't let this little setback stop me. I will work hard at my studies and make the most of every opportunity that comes my way," I declare confidently.

But how...? I wonder, at a loss for thoughts.

Even after all this, I am never angry at Shiva. My mother tells me to always have faith, and even more so in times of trouble. So that's what I do. With a smile on my face, I go about my day, doing odd jobs and running errands, gripping the dream of going back to school in my head and keeping my heart steady. The fire burns still, no matter how slow.

SAVINGS ACCOUNT

A*aj aasman boht saaf or neela hai*… (Today the sky looks really blue and wide, like it's been washed clean…)

I'm lying on this green field where I have been coming every single day to watch the aeroplane pass over me. Yeah, you heard it right. I am here, lying right beside the barricade that has a clear sign saying: NO TRESPASSING.

Right, I have clearly trespassed, like many times before. But before the guards know and run after me, I will be far, far away from here… shooo…! Phew! Like a plane, I will vanish into thin air. They won't know where to look for me. It's the same Tom and Jerry situation every single day, only they have never caught me. They try to, but they can't. I am too fast. My friends say I am faster than Usain Bolt. Only if I could test it out. I have outrun every single person in my life up until this point. I will be lying if I say I don't have the "training".

Kya hua? Soch me pad gye? (Hey, what's up? You look like you're deep in thought.) Hmph, you will understand soon. But first, let me enjoy my view.

This place is very close to the airport. I always climb the huge fence and make my way closer to the runway. It's nothing compared to what I have seen in all my life of thirteen years. It's a joke what they do in the name of security. They say this airport was built with over 30,000 crore, *thoo!* What a grand joke.

Security ke naam pe ye sasta fencing or chaar-panch overweight guards. Bhaag toh paate nahi agar kuch emergency ho bhi jae toh. (Some security this is—flimsy fencing and a bunch of out-of-shape guards! They'd be useless in a real emergency.) *Chee!*

Aah, I have this habit of spoiling my good mood sometimes. I am here to watch my beloved aeroplanes fly over my head. And I have been lying here under the scorching sun for what? It has been ten minutes already.

Oh how my digital watch glares in the sun! It's so awesome, honestly. Whoever had it before me lost a treasure. *But yahi zindagi hai, kisi ka fayda, kisi ka nuksan…* (That's how life goes, one person's gain is another's loss…)

Aa bhi ja… (Come, my heart's delight!) Yes! I can already hear the queen of my heart coming up. The ground is reverberating with her great might. Ooh! Look at the gravel, how they're dancing with each other. Wow! My heart is pounding! Come closer—want to know what I do? Whenever an aeroplane approaches and is about to take off, I put my chest on the ground and let the vibrations become one with my heartbeat. I feel my heartbeat getting lost in its great reverberation. It feels like I am part of some great music, some otherworldly symphony. It feels like I am one with something bigger, the field, the ground, the runway, yes, even the earth itself, perhaps the air too. I feel one with it. I feel big, and I lose myself. This is the feeling I enjoy the most—oops, second most. The best is yet to come…

Here comes my queen, spreading her wings. As she lifts from the ground, the air becomes her adversary and tries to stop her, but she fights through and spears through the air like she's supposed to. There she comes…

I fall down on my back to witness her soar… What a beautiful, majestic view… I get to see this for a few moments only, so I will turn my thoughts off. Here she comes, taking over the sun now… Breathtaking! Simply breathtaking!

My queen is right here, right before my eyes, above me, as I watch her fly away to some faraway land.

The air will hit me now, like a slap!

Oh! I will come here again, probably tomorrow, if I miss her too much. And guess what? Like there are four queens in cards, there are plenty of queens here too (wink wink).

I love how they take off, grow in size, make the roaring sound while moving through the air, and cast their shadow over me, blocking the sun. A mesmerising and magical sight to see the planes glide mightily through the clear, blue sky. While lying on the ground, as I look at them, I am filled with a rush in my heart. My blood suddenly feels like it's going to fill my heart completely, and my heart will burst. It's so exciting to me.

And you know what? The one thing that gives wings to my imagination is the fact that there are people of all nationalities sitting inside. I wonder where they might be going … Malaysia? Thailand? Singapore? Who knows … where the road goes…? A rush of excitement fills me as I imagine the adventures and destinations awaiting those on board.

My queen has left the runway and her king behind. *Ab mera yaha kya kaam?* (What do I do now?) I jump off the ground in Bruce Lee-style and make my way towards the fence I climbed to come here. Oh oh! Here they come whistling… What!? They have a dog too this time? But little do they know, these dogs are nothing compared to this slumdog right here…

These dogs don't know what it is to exist without a proper shelter, or without food. These dogs are trained and fed abundantly; they don't know what it is to stay hungry for hours searching for food. They don't have the training that survival has given me. These foolish puppies can't get me.

Here they come, closer and closer … and bam! I hit the fence and climb it like a spider. These puppies probably don't even know what a spider is, but they have seen a human-sized spider today.

Eh he he! Gotcha! Na, na, na, na, nah! Go eat dust, puppies! And you, lazy excuse of guards!

I jump down from the two-metre-high fence and land on my feet. I look back at the losers to relish the defeat on their faces. And now, it's time to bid farewell. I salute them for trying to give me competition, and then I turn back to the road where I came from.

"Oye! Chhotu!"

I look back and see what! My digital watch! One of the guards has it, damn it! He is shining the glare at me and teasing me. But it doesn't matter, I shall come back to take what's mine.

You must be wondering who this charming young fellow is. Hi, my name is Jitu, because I always win no matter what. But some ignorant people call me Chhotu at times.

I do rag-picking as a job. That's my daytime job; my night shift requires me to work at a *theka*, where I serve drunkards and get my dinner too. Don't judge me, I do whatever I can to get by. No, not just get by, I do whatever I can to make sure that I get rich before I turn eighteen. Right now, I am fourteen and I wish to be the richest fourteen year old.

Right from the beginning, from my childhood, I was convinced that to earn even a bit of respect in this world, one has to be rich—filthy rich. And that is exactly what I am going to be. I don't like this whiny culture of going to school, getting an education, and then working a 9-5 job to become a servant. No, I shall be nobody's servant. I shall build an empire. And I am working towards it every single day, every hour, every minute of my life. Some people from organisations and NGOs come and tell me that I should get admission in their schools or go to those government schools where kids like me study. But every single time, I tell them my conviction clearly.

Once, there was a Madam ji in a nicely-draped formal type of saree and a pair of goggles with a long string attached to it so they wouldn't get lost. She came up to me with a huge pile of papers—I hear they call it a file. Yes, she came up to me with that and then fixed her glasses a little, taking a long look at my filthy clothes. I was doing my job! I was rag-picking. I wished she would fix her nose too. Because it was always a little scrunched when she came to see us kids in the slum area. I don't know if somebody was making her do that, or if she was not getting paid enough. Anyway, she scrunched up her nose again and said to me, "Where are your parents?"

I too was clueless about that. Where are my parents? I don't know. Am I supposed to know, though? I mean, I was found crying in a garbage can on a rainy night. Some priest found me and took me to a local orphanage. They kept me there for as long as they could, and then one day, I ran away. I found this business where other kids like me picked rags and waste material from the streets and took it all for recycling in exchange for daily wages of about 100–150 rupees. I was happy with the money because it allowed me to have some change in my pocket and save some of it too.

"*Pata nahi* (Don't know)," I said plainly.

"*Or kon hai tumhare sath?* (Who else is with you?)" she asked.

"God."

"*Kya?* (What?)"

"*Jiska koi nahi hota uska bhagvaan hota hai* (If you have no one else, God will be there for you)," I said confidently.

"*Ye sab chhod do or hmara school join kar lo* (Leave all this and join our school)," she said, unamused by the confidence and charm with which I was talking to her.

So, as I had said, I make my daily wages doing rag-picking. I am saving it all for my future. And what are the other kids doing? Going to school, and for what? To become cockier servants? *Chahe kuch bhi ho* (Come what may), they will remain servants. After finishing their studies, they will become corporate or government mazdoors, wearing their suits and ties, acting like they are better than any of us. They have their parents telling them to do the same. Good for them, *par apna kaam nahi chalega. Apne sapne bade hain, sir pe maa baap ka saya nahi or time ki kami hai* (But that's no good for me. My dreams are too big, I don't have my parents' support, and there's never enough time). So, I have to do whatever I can to make my dreams come true.

And I told her the same. I said to her, "I am not interested, Ma'am, I want to make money so I can support myself and stand on my own feet. School won't put food on my plate or keep a roof over my head."

And then, I don't know why, she gave me a deathly stare, as if I had said something against her personally. She stared at me for long with a hard look, as if her eyes were going to pop out. I bet she was grinding her teeth too. But I didn't look away, nor did I look down. I kept looking at her as before, like an unassuming child.

I wonder what had offended her so much. Perhaps she had not expected a child of filth to be so outspoken, so full of life, so confident in himself. Perhaps she wanted to see a cry baby, desperate for help, for food and cloth, for the basic necessities of life. I was none of that. I stood tall and shone brightly despite the filth on my body, or more precisely, the filth in her own mind.

So why was she making faces every time she interacted with me? Wasn't she also a servant to her NGO or any other organisation that hired her? What was so filthy about me that she couldn't even look at me like I was a human? It felt like her eyes didn't want to waste themselves on me for even a moment. It seemed she did not want to be next to me. I could see it all.

And yet, she was there, God has his own ways of making things happen. Perhaps she was frustrated that I was in a better mood than her, given my circumstances. Perhaps she was not accustomed to voicing her opinions out loud with confidence. Perhaps she didn't have opinions that needed to be voiced out. Perhaps they were filthy.

And God was watching, He was making this situation happen. Just the way I was found, even though I was clearly discarded by my birth parents. I was found! I was given life at that moment.

And for that reason, I have faith in the Almighty. I have faith that somehow, someday, I shall be found again. And I will get my big break. That is the reason why I walk with my head held high. So what if I make money by picking up the waste that people leave on the streets and roadsides so carelessly? Are they not the ones responsible for it? I just do my duty to the nation by picking these waste and rags and sending them off for recycling. And I see no shame in it.

As she did not stop staring at me with hate, with the eyes of an assassin, I asked her, "What? Cat got your tongue?"

At that, she rushed up to me, as if she was going to slap me then and there, and suddenly realised she was standing in the same filth as I. And as God had conspired so, she was standing right there amidst the pile of dirt and waste. She realised that too late—her perfectly draped and pleated saree had gotten soiled. She must have thought she didn't want to get her hands dirty by slapping a child of dirt. So she spat beside me and left, muttering something.

Perhaps these people don't know that we are not just born in this filth, we are sustained by it too. Nobody wants this filth, nobody wants to touch the dirt, but here it is, providing for me. The great divine Mother doesn't discriminate. She provides for all. We are all her children. And even though I don't know my birth parents, I know the divine mother who fills me with enthusiasm for the day ahead.

But aren't we all born in the filth, though? When a baby comes out of its mother's womb, where does it exactly emerge from? It's not exactly a pristine five-star hotel, is it? The baby is born all covered in the filth of its mother that the nurses then clean up. They clean up the baby too. We are all born in filth. So why was she scowling at me?

Just for that reason, I decided I would not go where she was trying to take me. I would not go to a place where there were people like her who looked down on kids born in filth. I would never—I could never. *Mere zameer ne mujhe ijazat nahi di* (My conscience wouldn't let me). I would never survive on their alms. I, Jitu, born in the filth of divine Mother India, shall be sustained by her.

So I am happy here, picking rags and saving up for my business. I wonder if that woman realises that I am not just a rag-picking kid in filth; I am serving my nation, I am keeping her clean, I am doing the job that destiny has given me by birth, and I am doing it with all my dedication. I'm not sure about her dedication, though.

Night is creeping across the horizon and I need to tidy up so I can go and serve the customers at the bar. What I do is, I go to a public tap in my slum and get myself washed up. The aunties are always there with their pails to nag and complain about their turn to fetch water in the evening, but I take my time. They have a house to go back to after fetching water, but where do I go? All I have is this, and I sleep at the bar—that too for just four hours. Sleep is for the weak.

After I have managed to wash myself and changed into the only pair of clean clothes I have, I go to work—serving the drunk. I keep my day's earnings in a pot I have hidden somewhere I cannot tell for my own security. I cannot wait to turn 18 and open my own bank account. Then I won't have to worry about keeping my money safe. I keep some of it on me as cash and then go about my way. On my way to the bar, I take an e-rickshaw. I feel he might even recognise me as a regular by now. He drops me off at the bar every night.

One day, he even asked me out of curiosity, "*Arey chhotu*, why do you go to the bar? Do you drink *abhi se*, as a child? *Ye sab mat karo beta, zindagi kharab ho jaegi ek bar lat lag gayi toh.* (Hey Chhotu, why do you go to the bar? Do you drink already, even as a kid? Don't do all this beta. It'll ruin your life once you get addicted.)"

To which I chuckled and said, "No, Uncle, I do not drink. I go there for work. I wait tables there."

He still looked at me with suspicion. Anyway, I gave him the fare and went about my business. The harmful effects of alcohol are well known by me. In the slum where I live, the husbands beat up their wives and make a lot of noise after coming home drunk. I see them at the bar too, but they never recognise me as they are just there, loaded with cheap alcohol, half-awake half-alive, barely able to open their eyes. Yes, I serve them alcohol and other snacks that they ask for. I bring them with utmost dedication. Some of them know me, as they see me there regularly. They call me Chhotu, and I don't contest that. I try telling them my name every now and then, but they are just drunkards; all they can remember is alcohol. It happens sometimes that when I fetch the bill, they shoo me away or try to make a scene.

"Put that in the log…" they suggest often. But the owner of the bar asks me to be strict with them and demand for the bill to be paid in full. If I don't do that, I will be punished.

So, what am I, a fourteen-year-old teenager, left with? Man up! That's what I do. I, just a kid, man up in front of drunkards who are much older than me. Well, I try as best as I can. So, my employer, the owner of the shop, is pretty happy with me. He lets me stay the night there in the storeroom. That is where I sleep. And I have no complaints about it. I get a good sleep of three to four hours. This is my life here, and I am just waiting to turn 18, when I can deposit all my saved-up money safely in a bank account.

I may seem to have a work schedule in place now, but things weren't the same always…

There was a time when I didn't even have enough spare change to get myself one square meal a day. It was tough, but I was not going to give up that easily. I was determined to not end up like some of my childhood friends who had fallen for the wrong things in order to survive.

I know it might be a huge taboo for some, or maybe not, but some of my friends got addicted. Yes, in their formative years, when they should have been learning the ABCDs and the क ख ग घs in school, they were getting high without even knowing what 'being high' meant. These were children who were just like me—they had no one to feed them, to teach them, or to guide them on the right path.

They were just at the receiving end of the harshest realities of life. In the chilly winters of December, when the cold would get unbearable and bone-chilling, we wouldn't have any blankets or even a piece of cloth to separate the cold hard ground from our feeble, skinny bodies. The harsh winter is when so many of us are forced to resort to the use of alcohol, smoking weed and even some stationery items that we find on our own in public schools. What would a kid like me, suffering from the wrath of scarcity, winter, hunger, and a cold world, do? That's what my friends did. They got high, their eyes didn't look straight, and their voices were distracted, even their thoughts were.

What can such a kid think of while being high and on a trip? Perhaps they wonder about their parents, maybe they meet them, talk to them, or—or, they imagine themselves cuddling up in a warm bed with hot soup on the side table. Perhaps they imagine themselves laughing and making merry with their friends. It must be a beautiful world, so different and so magical. Up above the nightmare that their reality can be. It must feel great to not be aware of any of this … no cold, no tears, no shivering, no one rebuking, no world to remind us of everything that we don't have…

And then, bam! Reality hits you harder than it ever did before when the high turns into your lowest-ever low. No, I want it back! Everything hurts! The cold is back, hunger is gnawing at me, my body is still frail, I am still a street dog…

I have seen many of them get wasted away just like that. I don't judge them for having given in to the temptation. It's way too harsh, but I've decided that this pain is worth it if I want to make it out alive and sane. I can't let myself be reliant on this fleeting ecstasy and forget all about the ground reality. So I choose to rely on other means to stay alive.

It messes with your head—grabbing something from someone drowning in abundance, knowing they won't even notice, but still feeling your gut twisting with guilt. But guess what, compulsions of survival eat at you worse. So I did for some time what you would call stealing, just to keep myself going. Even though I was able to get by, I still felt bad and sorry for my other friends who chose to lose themselves in an illusion rather than to run their feet on the burning ground. I don't blame them, neither should you. Out of the little that I used to get for myself or—in layman terms—steal for myself, I made sure I shared it with my friends. I had little and I was happy to share; they had a lot, yet they could never share with a kid like me.

Let me tell you exactly who I am talking about, and where I stole from. You see, in the winters, there's one industry in India that just keeps on getting bigger and bigger exponentially—yeah, the big fat Indian wedding industry, that's what I am talking about. So, every now and then I would get ready in a clean shirt and a pair of borrowed jeans and sneak into one of the weddings. Sometimes I was able to get in without being recognised, but at other times, they would stop me right at the entrance, suspecting I was someone they had seen before. Kids like me, who looked like me, were strictly prohibited and shooed away like street dogs. And that is who we are, right? Street dogs. And if I have to be a street dog, I will make sure I am the darndest and the most formidable of them all. I will make myself so big and better than everyone else that it will be harder and harder for them to shoo me away. This is the promise I have made to myself. And I will fulfil it no matter what…

AN AWAKENING

As soon as I open my eyes, I find the terrace leaking. Oh, not just leaking, but pouring, as it's raining cats and dogs. It is the month of July, and after a long fortnight or so of hot summer days, the rain is finally there. I can't help but observe that the seasons in India now are not as regular and on time as they used to be. Everything used to happen on time back then—when it was time for summer, the dry and suffocating summer would be there, when it was time for the rains to come, they would come and perform their duties. Then autumn would follow suit and the days would become magical and calmer. The wind wouldn't be humid, and just right to soothe the mind. And in winters, the cold would chill our bones to the marrow.

That should be the way of nature—on time and doing what it's supposed to do. I believe that just like nature, all of us—being part of the same nature—are supposed to have cycles and follow a pattern. And if not that, we are supposed to follow nature in her footsteps. Like the seasons, we humans have our seasons too, like, our different ages. There is a time to wake up and there is a time to sleep; when we don't take care of the time in our lives, life stops taking care of us. I try a lot to keep my life the same way. I try to wake up at a certain time and go to bed early after finishing my homework and revision for the day. But it turns out, life doesn't care about our little plans at all. I take a look at the plastic watch I had bought for 50 rupees at a mela near our house, it shows 3:30 in the morning. I am supposed to be asleep by now, but the stormy rains have decided otherwise.

"I've asked you so many times to get the roof fixed, but now look! Your lazy arse cannot fix anything!" I hear my mother yelling at my father, who scratches his head, unable to think of what to do in the situation. The rain-bullets hit our faces; sleep drifts away from my eyes as I realise my books might get wet in the rainstorm. Instantly, I get up and scramble to the rescue of my books. They have some water droplets over them which I wipe away immediately.

"Why can't you listen?"

My mother kicks my father, who lies on a bedsheet, drunk to such an extent that even the pelting rain can't wake him up. So, she has to kick him. After a kick or two, he opens his eyes and groans, "What are you doing?!"

Tired of yelling, she says for the last time, "Can't you see how bad it is? Our roof is leaking! You were supposed to fix it."

"So am I supposed to fix it now?" he asks as he stands up unsteadily on his wobbly feet, taking the support of the chipped wall. He then covers his eyes with his hand and peers at the leaking roof, which is just a covering of tin shed, threatening to fly away at any moment due to the billowing winds. A rain-bullet strikes his eye and falls back down.

"Ow!"

Quick on my feet, I rush to support him.

"Are you okay?" I ask, and he shirks me away to say, "Hey, Chhotu, you are not a little child anymore. Why don't you take care of such small chores?"

Yeah, my parents did not even bother to give much thought to what to call me. So they settled with Chhotu.

My mother raises her eyebrows and tells him, "How can you be like this? Chhotu's tenth boards is coming up. He studies hard every single day. If he starts doing all these chores, what are you going to do? You are the man of the house. It's your responsibility to take care of your wife and kids. Such a coward, asking his son to fix the roof."

My morning alarm rings soon—it is 4 in the morning. My parents keep fighting, and there are no signs of the argument calming down.

"Why don't you teach your son these little things?"

"He is your son too!"

"I am going up there to fix the roof," I assert, and the quarrel stops at once.

"Why you? It's raining heavily up there."

I say nothing and climb up. It is time for me to start my day and then get to study. But it is not going to be possible as long as my parents keep fighting. When I reach the roof, I find that it is raining too heavily to see clearly. I somehow force my eyes open. It is still dark and the sun hasn't risen yet.

There is no time for me to even wish for a torch in my hand. I don't wait for my eyes to adjust to the dark and try to feel where the leak is with my hands. My hands look for the waves on the tin shed and trace the place where it is not touching the roof. I realise that the violent winds, that are still very much there, have turned it over to the side. There is nothing but iron wires to keep it in place. I find the wire and wind it back into place.

"*Abhi thik hai!* (It's working now!)" my mother called out from below.

I heave a sigh of relief and carefully climb down the ladder, keeping myself from slipping in the pattering rainfall. The raindrops constantly hit my eyes, and I somehow manage to keep my foot where it should be. At the bottom of the ladder, my mother is there, holding it steady. It breaks my heart to see that she is drenched just like me, while my father has already gone back to sleep in the corner. He is already snoring too. It seems as if he never really woke up. Anyway, I clamber down the wet ladder and my mother wipes my face with her pallu.

"*Shabaash! Tera baap toh ghode bech ke so gaya, jaane de usko. Hum dono milke garam chai pite hain. Thik hai?* (Attaboy! Your dad's out cold, forget about him. Come on, let's have some hot chai. Sound good?)" she says, trying to cheer me up.

Having lost about half an hour of my allotted time that is supposed to be dedicated to my studies, I am reluctant to waste another second.

"*Aap pi lo, maa, mujhe padhai karni hai. Naha toh maine lia hi hai.* (You go ahead and drink it, Maa. I've got to study. And I've already taken a bath anyway.)"

I pick up my books and sit down in the only corner that isn't crowded or ambushed with goods. I am relieved to see that my books are all nice and crisp, like new, just the way I kept them throughout the year. I turn on the bulb and feel relieved to see that at least something is working fine in my household. I forget everything and immerse myself in the study of mathematics, my favourite subject. It gives me a thrill every time I crack a tough math problem. It is a sure shot way to bring a smile to my face.

"Yes!" I exclaim, elated to have cracked another one, unaware of when my mother had come there. She has been watching me from behind intently, smiling to herself.

"*Ye le, chai pi le. Kitni mehnat karta hai mera beta. Bhagwan tujhe tarakki de.* (Here, have some chai. You work so hard, my son. May God bless you with success.)"

She puts her hand on my head, then leaves for the kitchen. I smile back and pick up the tea cup, it has ginger in it—a relief after being hit by the smashing raindrops. I am cold and shivering a little. At least the roof isn't leaking anymore. I keep studying there for three hours, and then it is time to leave for school. I get ready and polish my shoes to a shine, and my mother comes to the gate to see me off with an umbrella. It is still raining. I ask her to keep it as she might need it later, or father might, but she smiles to herself and says, "Look at your drunk father, he is still fast asleep. And he will stay this way for the whole day. You go to school, okay?"

She then gives me a peck on my head and hands me the umbrella.

As I step out of the door, I meet my neighbourhood friends. We are a group of three, never scared of studying continuously for the whole night. Yes, together, we are the three musketeers who ace every single exam. We are the proud toppers of our school. Me, Bunty, and Rahul. Our strides are filled with great confidence as we walk to the school. The neighbours look at us with a sense of pride and hopeful eyes. We have big dreams for our futures. I want to be an Air Force pilot, Bunty wants to join the prestigious Indian Navy, whereas Rahul wants to go around the world.

"But how are you going to get the money necessary for it?" we used to ask him with curiosity, because as far as our lifestyle was concerned, our parents had taught us to study hard to earn money and lead good, independent lives for ourselves.

Most of the people in our area are either labourers, rag pickers, small shop owners, feriwallahs, or professional drunkards like my father. He is also a construction worker, but he has taken the wrong support of addiction to get himself through the day. With his frail looking body, it has become even more of a struggle for him to keep up with his job. Mother tries to convince him to open a tea shop or another street food shop, but he keeps on procrastinating. He hasn't even bothered to go back to his work for two—not days—weeks! He just stays inside the house and lets the booze make him forget everything. And then he goes into a deep slumber. So, as the only child of my parents, I want to become independent, and not just that, I want to be respected in our society too.

Hence, the dream to become an Air Force pilot. And why not? I have the height, the physique (which I will work on every single day, until I die!) and then I'll study hard to make sure I ace that exam. I get my general knowledge from my school teachers who are generous enough to lend me the daily newspaper and all the general knowledge books. I feel incredibly blessed, and I obviously share them with my buddies.

It's a ritual for all of us to sit down and do group study. Yeah, I know what you must be thinking—what a bunch of boring young folks! And I am not denying the fact that we are, in fact, boring. It's just that we are so focused on making our goals come true that we never even think of doing the normal childlike stuff that our peers do. We study in school, make sure to answer all the teacher's questions, and then we study in the nearby library till evening.

Lunch? No, sir, we would rather use the midday meal time to study. I know it's a bit too much, but that is only because we want to fulfil our desire to become successful and respectable so badly that we cannot even think of anything else. What else should we do? This is our way of life—when we grow up, we don't want to end up like our parents. We want our parents and everybody else to see that we made good of our lives and became something more, someone important.

Our class teacher, Mr Shah, is an amiable and easygoing man. He was the first one to encourage me to study hard and strive to become an Air Force pilot. I still remember that day as clearly as it had happened. I was writing an exam when Mr Shah had come to our class for the first time. I was busy writing my paper when he looked at me and asked, "You must be the topper of your class?" I was not into studies so much back then. All I ever thought about was how my life was full of pity, how my mother was almost always sick with worry about the family's future because her husband—my father—did not work at all. I have already told you everything about this, right? So I was like, okay, I am going to end up just like my father. And I was shrouded in a very gloomy perception of life.

I had no enthusiasm and excitement in life, because I never thought I could be any better. I was one of the kids who always used to sit on the last bench. Yes, I was a proud backbencher. I was all about coming to class just to grab my lunch, as they used to have good food and a nice menu. I enjoyed it thoroughly. Other than that, I hated being in the classroom.

Me and my then peers used to make fun of any teacher that came to teach us. I would talk back and crack jokes whenever a teacher tried to set me straight. I felt like a hero when everybody laughed at my jokes. I felt good when the teacher would give up teaching me anything and go back to the board to teach other students. Yes, that's how I was. I thought it was my utmost glory to make someone feel small. I thought it was my greatest achievement when nobody could tell me what to do. I enjoyed my reputation as the bad boy of the class. I enjoyed it so much that I walked with the gait of a king. That was my life, until the day Mr Shah came into my life. I don't know what he saw in me that day when I was writing my exam. I sure didn't know what I was doing, but I was trying my best to write as much as I could remember from my studies the previous night. I had just mugged it all up within two or three hours. And I had a good memory anyway. I was able to remember most of the stuff that was taught in my class, even though I was busy having fun simultaneously.

There were times when I used to get bored and tired of cracking jokes and having fun. In those moments, I would put my head down and listen to the teacher. I could remember each and everything I heard then. And that was what helped me during the exam.

Anyway, that day, I was busy making the diagrams and labelling them. And I was stunned to hear the question that Mr Shah had asked me. I could hear the kids around me snickering under their breath. I don't blame them, but for the first time, it felt bad. I knew they were laughing at me. I then knew what it must've felt like to be the teacher when they were laughing at her. I was the reason they had laughed at her, or maybe I wasn't. But then, I realised, it wasn't me that they were laughing at. It wasn't the teacher either.

They were the crowd; they made fun of everyone. It gave them a sick pleasure to make fun of people. Some time back it was the teacher, and that day, it was me. I understood everything in that one moment. He had only asked me a simple question. But I knew he was not joking with me. He was new to the school and knew nothing about my tricks and jokes. He was asking me that question genuinely. I could not have asked that question to myself in a million years, because I never thought that a nobody like me could be of any use to society or even my parents. I could never imagine that in my wildest dreams. I was so shocked to hear that question that a shiver went down my spine at that moment. And I remember it so clearly—it felt as if I had been awakened in that moment. I was clearly ashamed of having "no" as an answer to that question. I lowered my gaze and shook my head. The other kids now laughed openly.

The teacher shushed them then and there and looked back at me. He then asked me, "Do you want to become the topper?" Every bone in my body was somehow screaming: "Yes, yes, I want to be." I didn't want to be the joker the crowd laughed with and then laughed at later on. I didn't want to end up as someone who was the reason why someone got laughed at either. It was very clear to me. And also, I didn't want to be a part of the crowd either. All they knew about was laughing at someone. They always wanted someone to entertain them. Some days it was the teacher, and on other days it was me. At that moment it was me. So what was I left with then? What choice did I have? I knew at that moment the only choice left was to take a stand for myself and my future. And that's when I decided I wanted to be the topper of my class.

That moment with Mr Shah was enough for me to make a complete U-turn. He understood the sincerity and longing to stand out from my face. And that was the reason why he had asked me that question. And even though I didn't reply back to him, he gave me a nod and patted me on my back. I looked at my then friends—they were all laughing at me. I realised that they were not my friends either. I understood a lot of things in that one brief moment.

So, I wrote my exam, but I wished I could have done better. After I finished it, I picked up my bag and looked inside. There were no books in it—just a rough notebook. I had been carrying it for years. And it was still not complete with the study material because I only relied on my memory to write my exams, and even after that I was able to score a respectable 70% and above. I was sad to see the plight of my studies.

I took a look at my bag. It was filthy, and I had never cared to wash it. I then looked at my uniform—it was filthy too. *Oh God!* I thought to myself. Why had no one ever told me to wash my bags and take care of my books? Why had no one ever told me to keep my uniform tidy? Why had no one ever told me that I could be better too? I blamed everyone around me at that moment. I blamed my mother, my father, my teachers, my friends, everyone. I was so mad at the world for the first time in my life. I was so angry, and then it hit me. It wasn't the world that was at fault. It was me. Why did I not have a bigger vision for myself? Why did I not have any big dreams? I realised that the toppers of my class, who I had been making fun of all these years, were all winners in my eyes. I had to become friends with them. And that's when I approached Rahul and Bunty. I extended my hand to them and said, "Hey, I want to be your friend. Can we?"

They looked at me with surprised expressions for a moment, but then they must've been getting late for the library. Upon realising that, they said, "Okay, you can be." Rahul took my hand and greeted me. And then I shook Bunty's hand. They smiled at me with so much sincerity that it touched my heart. I felt like I had done something right in my life.

I accompanied them to the library. I watched how they made notes and studied the ones the teacher gave us. I had never bothered to jot down notes myself, as I was confident that I wouldn't forget anything. But I realised the sincerity and dedication with which these two were making their notes. I started to realise so many things that were amiss in my life. I didn't even have a proper sharpened pencil to make notes with. Rahul was kind enough to lend me one. But he was quick to warn me too: "Hey, remember to bring it back tomorrow. It is the only other pencil I have."

I made a little face, but it wasn't his fault that I didn't even have a nice pencil. So I nodded. I wrote everything down with focus by watching them. I noticed they recited everything they wrote so that they'd be able to remember it clearly while writing the exam. I looked at their handwriting and it was as if they had some kind of magic in their hands. I was impressed. I was clearly living under a rock to have never realised how awesome these folks were. Honestly, I realised how big a fool I had been all this time. Anyway, I studied with them till late in the evening. And when I finished, I was surprised to see that my notebook was about to be filled to the last page. It had taken two years for my notebook to be half-filled with school notes.

"Whoa!"

I was mesmerised at my own ability to do something amazing. I still remember how it felt—my chest was filled with so much air. For the first time, I felt I could control the direction of my life. When I went back that day after studying for hours, I was greeted by my anxious mother crying at the gate. She was sitting with her head down. Some other neighbour aunties were trying to calm her down.

I went running to her and asked, "What happened, Maa?"

She looked up at me with wide, startled eyes, as if she had seen some ghost. I couldn't understand what was going on, and then she cried even more. The neighbour aunty told me that my mother was weeping because she thought I had gone missing. She had sent my father to look for me.

"Ma, stop crying."

I wiped her tears and said, "Ma, I was in the library."

She could not believe it of course, and then I opened my notebook and showed her the notes I had made. For the first time in my life, I saw a big smile appear on my mother's face. Then she wiped her tears and hugged me. "I am proud of you, my son," she said.

"Ma, I will fix everything, don't worry ever again."

DOLL

I love the sound of my mother's *payal*, a simple silver-coated anklet that tells me when she has woken up. The tinkling of the little bells on her feet brings our mud house alive. My mother is a hardworking woman; she wakes up early, sweeps the house, brings wood from the forest to prepare breakfast, and then washes the utensils. I sit at the threshold with my arms in my lap and smilingly watch her carry out her duties. I am mesmerised by her. What else can I do but watch my beautiful mother, wishing to become like her one day?

At times she looks at me and smiles, squeezing her eyes at me from afar. My heart flutters, and I laugh with joy every time she does that. My mother braids my hair into pigtails after oiling it well. She sews clothes for me—sleeveless tops and matching long skirts—from her old sarees. She lovingly puts a big red bindi on my forehead before I trot off to play with my friends.

Every girl in my friend group brings their own dolls, and we play with them under a banyan tree. With sticks and rags we create a dollhouse with rooms for each of our dolls. My friend Shikha is the only one with a boy doll, so the other girls, including me, are eager to marry ours with hers. Shikha is generous and lets us marry our dolls to her boy doll by taking turns. We stay out till late and when the sun sets, we walk back to our homes together. Back at home, I find my mother preparing dinner on the *chulha* (woodfire)—rotis with cooked vegetables from her little garden she maintains just outside our house. Upon reaching home, I realize my father has just come home as well. Amma tells me to wash my hands as the dinner is ready. The food is served hot, and it looks delicious. While I look at it admiringly, my appetite sharpening, my father puts his hand on my head and says, "You should start learning from your mother, Pooja. You should not be playing around with your friends; you have grown up now."

"But Appa, I am just fourteen years old, and I am the youngest in my friend group," I say with an adorable tone he loves.

Amma gestures to me to start eating and asks, "How is school now, dear? After finishing dinner, teach me some of your math tricks, okay?"

Amma knows how much I love math. In fact, I am really good at it. It is something that comes to me naturally. When I was just two years old, I learnt counting just by observation. I would see my father doing addition and subtraction at shops, and that's how I learnt it. I am always the first one to raise my hand and answer each question enthusiastically. I am a good student at all subjects, but an exceptional one at math.

I nod smilingly and start eating. "It's so good, Amma. How do you do this every single day? You make the best meals every day, Amma."

My mother smiles and looks at my father, who is eating silently. I wonder if he has come home tired, and if that's the reason why he is unusually silent. He is not even smiling at me every now and then.

"Ji, how is the food today?" Amma asks him, but he stays silent.

"Appa, is it not good? It's so delicious. *Hai na?* (Isn't it?)" I add, thinking this will get a reaction out of him.

My father stays quiet to finish his morsel and then says, "I finished work on the field early today and went to meet the boy's father. Vimal has passed his twelfth boards, and soon he will be joining his father's business."

My mother was not expecting such a reply. With the chulha still burning and the flames almost dying down, she gives him a puzzled look.

"Oh, don't act like you didn't know about this," my father scorns, putting the plate of food away.

I can't understand what is happening. I look at my mother, and then at my father quizzically.

"But what about her school? She is not ready," my mother says, putting the tongs aside. She looks upset yet respectful with a meek voice.

Something about the tension in the veranda tells me that it is I who is being talked about. But I can't quite grasp the whole gravity of the situation. All I can think of is, *Am I going to be taken out of school? Has the teacher complained to my father? Has Vimal told the teacher about me going to the mango orchard during lunch, without permission?*

Suddenly, the food tastes like rubber in my mouth, as if my taste-buds have died. My throat goes dry. I swallow the last morsel with much effort. I decide to keep quiet and listen to the conversation between the adults of the house.

"She can continue her schooling; nobody is saying anything against that. They even agreed to let her go to college after marriage."

"Marriage!" I blurt out without realising that it isn't just a thought in my head. I immediately feel guilty for talking between them. I have always been taught to stay quiet and meek like my mother and to never interfere when adults are talking. I put my head down, staring at the grainy floor with nervousness. I have always loved the idea of marriage, even all my girl-friends do. I just did not think that I would have to be married to Vimal, the puny guy with zero interest in studying. I am good at school, and definitely better than him. The idea of getting married to Vimal is mind-boggling. I carefully look at Amma with puppy eyes, pleading with her to put some sense into father's head. For all I care, she is the one who used to listen with banging laughter to my anecdotes of how some of the boys in my school were careless punks.

Father looks at me and says, "You're of age now, Gudiya. Schooling and all is fine, you don't even have to worry about getting a job after college. Vimal's father is well-off, you will have everything your heart desires. They have lands not just here, but in the neighbouring village as well. You are so lucky, Gudiya."

Nothing makes sense. Everybody knows that Vimal comes from a landlord family—that is the reason he never takes his studies seriously and even talks back to the teachers at school. He is a typical *dabangg* even at this young age. Moreover, he never respects girls and makes fun of their braids and the fit of their salwar kameez uniform. The idea of spending my whole life with him gives me the ick—I want to puke.

"Let her finish school at least, she is such a good girl. All the chores of the house will distract her and make her feel tired. How is she going to focus on studying?" my mother says, ensuring the roti on the *tawa* doesn't get burnt.

I nod lightly. It feels like something inside me is dying, a feeling of total powerlessness. My father is the decision maker of the house, and whatever he says is *patthar ki lakeer* (carved in stone). I have seen my mother agreeing to everything he says without a question. This is the first time I have seen her "talk back"—something frowned upon in our village.

My mother used to tell me stories of how her mother-in-law, my late dadi, was not very happy about my birth and wanted my mother to get rid of me, but because of a government campaign in the village during that time, they had decided not to. They wanted a son, but my father did not have the resources to have another child and support it. Nonetheless, after my dadi's passing, my mother focused all her attention on me. She did not know how to read, so I took it upon myself to help her read and write. We enjoyed our basic Hindi, English, and math sessions together, every day after dinner—until today.

Suddenly I feel the air is a little difficult to breathe in; it feels thick and heavy. A second later I realise that it is I who is breathing short, but my parents don't seem to notice it. They continue to disagree with each other. Suddenly, I feel my head becoming dizzy—due to the lack of oxygen perhaps—and the scene around me turning dark. I only hear a feminine voice screaming "Gudiya!" before I faint.

I am woken up by my mother at noon, way past school time. I immediately rise up, looking for my school bag and uniform.

"Take rest today. I have called and informed your teacher that you are not well. Lie down and have some milk." My mother's soothing voice calms me.

As I drink the milk, I study her face in an attempt to figure out the conclusion of their heated discussion, but her face looks pale and sad. I realise my father has not budged.

Life suddenly starts feeling like a cage. I don't feel like playing with my dolls anymore. What am I going to tell my friends when they come to fetch me in the evening? I can't focus on my books anymore, it all seems futile. My father's words keep ringing in my head: "You will have everything your heart desires… You don't even have to get a job…"

If all my needs are going to be provided for, what is the use of studying and trying to become a person of my own? What does that even mean, "*to become a person of my own?*" The most educated woman in my village is a twelfth pass, and she is married to a wealthy landlord's son in a city. Her mother often shows their pictures of being happily married to the village ladies, including my Amma. She indeed looks happy, with a nice car and a huge bungalow. I try to do the math in my head:

Let's suppose I study well and land a job—maybe as a lecturer. I am sure I can teach. At the entry level, I will have a pay of about fifteen to twenty thousand, as I once overheard my teachers at school. I will be in my twenties by then, and the last age of marriage in my village is twenty-three, which is frowned upon. So, even after landing a job, I won't have enough money to buy a car, let alone a huge car that Vimal's father owns. I surely won't be able to afford to buy a bungalow. So, what am I getting after becoming educated and independent? Certainly nothing that I can brag about.

This is when it starts to feel like a cage in my mind. I am unable to get past the one last question in my head—*what will I get after becoming educated and independent?*

I love my parents dearly, and despite their scarce means, they have given me everything that other children around me have. I can never do anything that will hurt their feelings. I am their beloved Gudiya, after all. I always want them to be happy, and I never want to be the reason for their suffering or worries. Because I am born a girl, I have become the cause of disagreement between them. I would rather hate myself than hate them for being bound to their circumstances. I have made up my mind to follow my father's wishes, so that the peace of the house is preserved. I breathe in and strengthen my resolve. I pass by the little mirror on the wall and go to see my mother. With wobbly feet I stand before her, pushing every ounce of the awareness of the question in my head: *what is the use of becoming independent and educated?*

"Amma, I am sorry."

My mother stops sewing the dress she is making for me and says, "What? Why are you sorry?"

"A fight happened between you and Appa because of me." Tears stream down my eyes despite my best efforts.

My mother shakes her head and wipes my tears with her pallu. She holds me close and kisses my forehead as consolation. She doesn't know how to reason with me or make me understand. Perhaps she doesn't understand what is going on either. My mother is a simple woman, she knows everything of the heart but nothing of the head. The head for her and the family is my father.

"Amma, Amma, I will do as Appa says. I am your Gudiya and nothing more," I force myself to say. The question still throbs loudly in my head, but I have no answer. If being educated means that I would have to break my parent's hearts, I would rather break my own. As that conviction sets in my head, I feel something inside me dying. I feel a gruesome silence inside my own being, as if I had killed something I didn't know about.

My mother keeps wiping away my tears and holds me tight. She weeps and says, "*Hey Ram, kya tune aurat ki zindagi banayi hai?* (Dear God, is *this* what you had in mind for a woman's life?)"

My tears dry up. I suddenly feel like a ghost after killing the question in my head. Every emotion in my heart and mind leaves, and I am faced with another question: "Does God create this pain? Is this pain only felt by women? Are all women doomed to cry the way my mother and I are?"

I feel furious at myself. Why another question? What is this thing inside my head that doesn't shut up? Even after having so much love for my parents, what is this thing that wants to question everything around me? I feel as if there is another me inside myself—she is different from my parents' daughter. Only that can be the reason why she doesn't care about my feelings for my parents.

"You should take some rest. I don't want you to skip another day of school," Amma says while I am still glued to her chest.

"Amma, why is school important?" I ask, knowing very well that my mother would be knowing nothing about it either.

"School is important, Gudiya."

"Why?"

"I just know it is. Becoming literate is better than staying *anpadh*."

"How is it better? All the educated women in our village end up with the same fates. They are all told to get married to a rich landlord. What is the use of their education?"

"Not all women, Gudiya."

I am left dumbstruck.

My mother continues, "There was a girl by the name of Swati, she was a friend of mine when I was about your age..."

Suddenly, the war inside me calms down as I listen to my mother with both head and heart.

"Swati was a brilliant girl just like you. She was not allowed to study by her family and was told that her ultimate fate was to get married to a guy of their choice."

"What?"

"Yes, but she was Swati, there was no one like her. She used to study her brother's book all on her own, without anyone to guide her. She somehow got her brother to stay shut about it. Whenever Swati came to meet us she would tell us about what she was going to do with her life: 'I think I am going to become this village's sarpanch one day. And I will make sure that this village becomes as progressive as England.' We all used to be amused at her words, thinking she was just boasting, as our fates were sealed by our families."

"Then what happened? Did she become a sarpanch?"

"She became something even she had not imagined. Swati had learnt all that a girl was supposed to—she knew cooking, sewing, tailoring, draping a saree, all the while home-schooling herself in secret. She was a hardworking one, and dedicated. With the basic addition and subtraction that she had learnt, she decided to meet with the neighbourhood tailor and offer to help him. He was reluctant in the beginning, but when she stated that she would help him double his earnings, he agreed. And with a commission of ten rupees on each finished clothing, she started sewing in her home."

"She had the mind of a businesswoman."

"Indeed, she brought home piles of clothes and sewed them, burning the midnight oil. When her family asked, she told them she was doing favours for friends. And they believed happily, thinking their daughter was dedicating herself to house chores."

"Smart."

"Yes, and she started saving up. I still remember that day—she had a divine glow on her face when she told me she was going to the city to explore the world. I thought she was going mad! Go to the city? Being a girl? All alone? Of course, she asked me to accompany her, to which I refused. I was too scared, you see. But I was there to see her off at the bus stop. I kept telling her, 'You are crazy! You are crazy! What if you are found out?!' And she replied in her same crazy tone, 'We will see.' I came running back home, keeping myself covered with a dupatta. And the next day, she was back. Without losing a single breath she talked of cars, huge buildings, massive shops, dummies wearing jeans and western clothing, women going to work, walking on the streets, laughing and eating freely, even at night. I felt as if she was talking about a movie she had watched. But it was all real."

My mother breaks into laughter, and I laugh with her. "So then, what happened?"

"Swati told me she had decided to move to the city. I knew her family would never allow it. She said she was willing to wait for the right time to come. One day, her parents told her that they had fixed her marriage to a boy from the city. When she told me about it, I remember being thrilled for her and telling her, 'This is even better. You wanted to go to the city, and now you are going to get married into the city!' But she did not look pleased."

"Why?!" I exclaim.

"Swati said she wanted to get a college degree first and then move to the city to make a life for herself. She was saving up through her little business to make that dream come true."

I stay silent, not knowing what to ask. My mother continues, "When she told her parents about it, they were furious and immediately asked her to get married instead."

"So? Did she listen?"

"Swati was sad to give up her little business and decided that the time indeed had come for her. She declared to her family and the society, 'I believe I can be as huge as Kalpana Chawla and P.T. Usha.' They laughed at her and called her crazy. Relatives and family members alike surrounded her constantly to make her agree to the marriage. When the boy's family heard about the hue and cry, he demanded to meet her. Swati, tired and hungry, said to him, 'I am a free bird, and I must fly.' The boy replied, 'But think about the society, your parents, they are getting worried for you. They only want to see you looked after.' Swati felt her heart become weak at the mention of her parents, but the voice inside was still strong, and she said with a weak voice, 'I must fly. I want to study, and I want to be a woman of my own. Then, I will happily marry you.' The boy saw the fire burning in her eyes, even though her face had gone pale. He felt ashamed of himself for not being as brave as her. He quietly listened to all the judgements coming from Swati's family and relatives and finally said, 'I will marry her, but only after she and I both stand on our own feet.' Swati felt relieved, and an emotion of triumph rushed through her veins. She tasted victory in that moment—a huge victory—to have her own struggle in life, so she might finally become who she dreamt to be."

Amma falls silent. I am too stunned to speak, but there is a different silence in my head now. It is not a ghastly silence like the earlier one, but a silence of satisfaction, contentment, relief at having all my questions answered while sitting in my mother's lap. I fix my gaze on Amma, who is regarding me curiously. I notice that the tears on my face have dried. The world around me feels different—I feel different. I raise my head from my mother's lap and whisper to her, "You were lucky to have such a great friend, Amma. I'm sure she made her dream come true."

My mother caresses my head and says, "Here, have some water. I have to prepare dinner."

"Yes, Amma, and I will study until dinner is ready. You make the best food." I give her a peck on her cheek and flutter away to solve math problems, now that my existential problems are all solved because of the woman named Swati. Because of her, I now know it is not about materialistic gains—bungalow, car, expensive furniture, or smartphones. The importance of education and being independent is to live a life of your own, not being tied down to circumstances and others' will, not being *majboor*—it's about becoming someone you are proud of. It's interesting and quite strange, though, how even after being such a powerful figure, Swati is unheard of in my village.

BESTSELLER

The earliest memories of my childhood are mostly dark. *Kabhi kabhi* (Often) I try and focus hard to remember something, but all I can see is darkness. So, was I born into a place of constant darkness? Or, is something wrong with my brain? I think the latter is more true. Though I can hear my own thoughts clearly, I find it extremely difficult to express them through words. I understand what words mean, I just cannot speak them. I fumble and stutter in the process, while the people around me laugh hysterically. They call me *goonga* and *pagal.* I am not crazy, but how do I tell them? So I stay quiet, what good is talking anyway? People say a lot but mean nothing—I hear them all day, blabbering and boasting about something they're going to do, something they did in the past, and even something they will never do. People sure speak quite a lot. Open any television channel, radio channel, social media—everywhere someone is talking, and then others are talking about them. At times, my head hurts a little just by thinking; it's unimaginable to me how they can go on and on with the muscles in their mouth.

The politicians talk in rallies, have heated discussions on news channels, and engage in a war of words in the Parliament. At the railway station, where I stay, all one can hear is the hubble-bubble and *faltu baatein* (nonsense talk). I'm sure they don't think of them as unimportant, but I have a knack for observing people, given the hundreds that pass me by. And from my keen observation, granted to me by my muteness, I can easily conclude that the most important folks tend to talk less. They rarely talk of their plans, let alone gossip about people; they're too focused on the future to talk of the past. They are the ones winning in life, silently.

So, my fifteen years at the railway station, spent trying to sell flowers and garlands as a mute person, have taught me the importance of silence—it is golden; it is even deafening at times. For someone like me who finds it easy to judge those who carelessly use and abuse the liberty of free speech, I do feel a great envy towards them. The railway station gets much quieter after midnight, and that's when I try to speak my thoughts. I take up this endeavour when my garland-seller friends have either drifted off to sleep or left for home. I don't have a home. I like to believe that this station is my home; my abusive friends, my family.

"Ha-hal-halo? Mm-my-eye-my nn-ay-mm-ah, ij Ch-ch-ch—"
"Oye Chhotu!"

Someone calls out, but I don't know which one of us he is referring to. Then it dawns on me, I am the only one awake and sitting upright. So, I look in the voice's direction. It is a guy—must be in his thirties—looking at me. I am too tired to go up to him, so I gesture to him to come to me with my index finger. He is clearly a little taken aback by my daring carelessness—eyebrows slightly raised, eyes growing wider with a puzzled expression—and I enjoy watching this reaction every single time. I may be a dumb kid, but I am a man of my word. I mean, I am a kid of my unshakable thoughts.

"*Maachis hai kya?* (Hey buddy, got a light?)" he asks me.

I look under the rag my friend was lying on and find the matchbox. He leans towards me with a cigarette in his mouth, expecting me to light it. But I am smarter than that; it is my speech-practising time, and I hate wasting this time. So, I fling the matchbox for him to catch. He looks at me with an expression of "how dare you!" I ignore him, and he begins to walk away.

Darn it! He's taking my matchbox!

The realisation dawns on me hard, but I cannot even cry out loud: "Oye, you ungrateful punk! Who do you think you are?! Bring that matchbox back, you useless freeloader!"

Yet again, like many times before, my rage quickly turns into helplessness. I just shrug it off and go back to my rehearsal. I have become better over the years; just five years ago I couldn't even force a sound out of my lungs. Before long, I fall asleep, dreaming of darkness.

Kya yaar, I was telling you about my earliest memories. There aren't any, because I was never really awake in the first place. What do I mean by that? My aunt, who connected me with a flower-seller to get rid of me once and for all, used to rage about how I was a burden all my life. And in those moments of rage, she often yelled, "*Tujhe metro station par nashe khila kar bheekh mangti thi teri maa. Agar maine tujh par taras na khaya hota, toh tu aaj bhi kahin pada hota.* (Your mother used to drug you and beg at the metro station. If I hadn't had mercy upon you, you would still be wasted.)"

Indeed, after my mother passed away due to pneumonia, my aunt took me in and slapped me into flower selling. My father was too busy drinking to care about my whereabouts. Initially, it was hard to stay awake without feeling weird, angry, and desperate for something to ease my mental frustration. Over time I realised that my mother's habit of drugging me was the reason why I felt like this. The feeling used to overcome me so much that I could not sit still and stayed fidgety. One day, I decided to give weed a try in an attempt to relive the euphoria and relieve the noisy frustration in my head. It was easy to arrange, and I felt high for some time, only to feel the same pit of darkness once again. My aunt was furious when she came to know about it through my cousin, and she slapped me until my ears bled. I am mute, I couldn't even cry out in pain. She did not beat me because she cared about me; she did that so I could make myself useful to her. I was to bring in the money from selling flowers.

I am thankful to her anyway. Because of her, I have given up drugs. I might never have a vibrant childhood memory to look back on, but I have the ceiling of this railway station over my head, the only memory good enough to remember. She has been kind enough to arrange a tutor for us who teaches us basic mathematics, Hindi, and English as well as he can on the weekends. She maintains that we are not to get admission in a school, as we have to bring in money. I have made it my life's purpose to learn everything I can from our tutor. I have learned more quickly than others how to write, and I find it extremely empowering. Though I am just a beginner, I have started to understand newspaper headlines. During breaks, I follow along and write above the headlines of scrap newspapers, trying to learn even faster. There are many books for sale outside these stations—they're called bestsellers. I know it because I can read it. These days, I have been having a dream at night, where I am one of the authors on the cover of these books.

SCHOOL IS FUN

"It's one of the most exciting days of my life. I'm going to school today," I say to my reflection in the mirror while combing my hair slowly with one hand and sleeking them out with another—no strays allowed, and my hair must shine like my shoes. I carefully take two more drops of oil in my little palms, rub them together, and finish off my slick look. It is now time to head to school in a completely new light.

Yes, it wasn't my first time there. I used to go to school every day, but with my father who is a gardener there. I accompanied him to help him, and he would take me so I could observe and learn as much as I could. It was a private school, and my father couldn't afford to enrol me there as a student. It was my mother who had insisted that I wouldn't be enrolled into a government school. She wanted me to attend a school of a "greater standard". I don't know what that means, but I guess it is about the shiny cars, bikes, scooters, and some bicycles that the students come in. Perhaps, it is their rich English speaking abilities or their well-off parents. I guess "standard" is a mix of it all. My father was a simple man; he never thought about standard, status and class when it came to children. He fondly used to say that each child is a representation of the Almighty. So, he didn't give it a fight and agreed to my mother's wishes. However, he could not pay the high fees, so he insisted that I learnt as much as possible from observation until he could afford the fees.

Until today, I went to school with my father before the teachers, students, and the Principal even set foot on the premises. The guard was the only one there to greet us on our arrival. At sharp 6 in the morning, we tended to the greenery spread around the building on each floor. It was hard work going to all four floors and watering the plants, which I did against my father's wishes. I could not let him be stressed early in the morning, so I asked him to stick to the ground floor garden and the field. I challenged myself to finish watering the plants within half an hour each day. Yes, sprinting and running around the school without entering a single classroom. One teacher who arrived early to prepare his lessons for the day often called out to me, "Oye Chhotu! Bring me a glass of water."

Yes, I happily served as a waiter for him because he let me sit beside him for some time and listen to him speak about his subject. Rachit Sir knew of my circumstances, and he took pity on me. I was a shy kid and never bothered to correct him and tell him my actual name, which is Fauji. I was given this name because my father dreamt of serving in the army but couldn't. Anyway, I listened to Rachit Sir as he read out his notes to me—I understood some of it, but I kept nodding and never raised a question even if I had doubts. Besides, I had to run back to water the plants and help my father.

It was my father's responsibility to get the garden cleaned up and ready before the Principal arrived. He was a tall and sharp-looking fellow in his sixties, with a nose that never looked down. He always had the same stern expression, as if he were a statue that was magically given the ability to walk. With his hands behind his back and an upright posture, he surveyed the entire school before the students arrived. My father always told me to never appear in front of him and sit in the canteen. I asked him why, but he never answered. I thought it was because I could never keep myself from giggling after seeing his mannerisms.

When I wasn't tending to the garden with my father, I used to stay in the canteen—not to just sit there and gawk at the students, though. My father had asked me to help with serving the students. Raju Uncle, the canteen owner, knew my father well and always greeted him with a smile. I helped him in the canteen during lunch hours, which was a total frantic situation. I loved everything about this school, and even though I never got the chance to sit in a classroom, I always imagined it to be a fun experience. So why were the children always so happy during the lunch breaks? Some of them rushed to the canteen before the lunch bell could ring! What was so hateful about learning that they could not help but escape at the drop of a hat? If I were given the chance, I would never get tired of learning about the world, history, the earth, environment, literature, current affairs, you know. I, Fauji, served at the canteen. The children were completely chaotic, and I used to be amused to see their energy. In an instant, five students would give their orders and I had to carefully listen and serve it to them. While Raju Uncle was busy on the grill preparing hot burgers and sandwiches, I was entrusted with handing them to the right students. Raju Uncle knew I had trouble taking so many orders at once, so he guided me. I was always amazed by his ability to remember. Anyway, I was happy to serve with a smile, and I am proud that I never made any mistake. Over time, I developed an ear for the conversations between the students. They talked about their teachers, spread gossip about their fellow students, and only a few discussed their subjects. I admired from afar and felt amazed—how great school life was!

My day went by like this, helping father, Raju Uncle, and watching the kids have a great time. They talked to me sometimes and wondered why I didn't go to school. I told them honestly, "Amma doesn't want me to go to a government school."

"Then why don't you get admission here? We will have such fun together!" said one of the students who was just my age. He and I had become great buddies over time. Siddy, his friends called him.

I was dumbfounded when asked why I didn't get admission there. I knew I should be truthful, but something inside me felt uneasy. As I was nervously contemplating the answer in my head, I looked at their well-kept uniforms, shiny shoes, perfect tie-knots, and clean nails. I was suddenly aware of why I could not go with these kids. I felt small. I just smiled and decided not to answer them. The conversation steered to another subject effortlessly. But I was still stuck with this pinching feeling in my gut that made me want to run away and hide somewhere.

While the world around me went on just like it did every other day, I felt my world grow dark all of a sudden. Wherever I looked, I was made aware of this striking juxtaposition of "them" versus "me". I was not supposed to be there. I felt out of place. While serving the kids, I glanced at my own clothes—a cotton shirt my mother had pressed with great care, that had been sullied by countless washes. It was tight on my chest as well. I had no shoes and only flotter sandals that my father had bought for me two years ago.

Raju Uncle noticed the change in my pace. He said, "Chhotu! Beta burger serve *karke do* (platter it up.)" A strange thought bubbled up in my head: *My name is Fauji, not Chhotu.* A fiery feeling rose in me—every bit of my body was burning. For the first time I felt anger at not being called by my own name. I felt the shame inside me turn into a deep resentment for everything and everyone around. I suddenly hated these faces; I hated their gossiping; I hated their carefree laughter; I hated their smugness; I hated that they didn't have to serve, that they were the ones being served. I hated this building; I hated myself for serving them. I could hear Raju Uncle say something in the background, but it was all muted. My being was burning with a feeling I didn't understand. Suddenly, I felt something hot on my feet—I had dropped the burger. I looked down and up at the people staring at me. Before they could look away and go about their lives, something inside me decided to run away.

I was running, hyper aware of the eyes on me. The tall and short figures around me were shadows I desperately wanted to dodge. Everything became blurry as I ran across the corridor—and all of a sudden, I bounced against something. When I retracted my face from it, I realised I had bumped into a huge flabby belly. I pulled back with the support of my little hands. All of a sudden, everything went silent. It was too silent—I may have heard some gasps. When I looked up sheepishly to see whom I had bumped into, I felt my blood run cold. Mr Prateek, who never looked down, was gawking at me through his chained glasses.

I was too stunned to keep running. I was too stunned to say sorry. I just looked up with bated breath. I knew everyone was waiting for me to get reprimanded. I was waiting as well. For a moment, I thought I might just run away, but before I could, he sighed. I wasn't expecting that. I was expecting a loud scolding, an open lecture on discipline in the corridors. I knew about it because I had seen it happen before with the students.

But he did none of that, he just … sighed! That was completely against his reputation. Every time I looked at him, I could sense he walked with an air of superiority like no other, with his nose held high. I looked into his eyes and realised he was not angry at all about my silly blunder. Relieved, I regained my senses back and stepped back.

"S-sorry, sir," I said. I knew better words like 'apologise', but my hesitation rendered me the good old 'sorry'.

He stayed quiet, looked at me with a pitiful expression, and started walking, adjusting his glasses. I was almost taking a deep breath in relief when I heard a stern voice say, "To my office, right now."

Just when I thought I was done for the day. My head hung low as I walked behind him. Inside my head, I was lamenting the turn of events.

What did I just do? Father always asked me to stay away from him, and now this? Well done, Fauji.

I was hoping my father wouldn't know about this. As soon as the peon opened the door to the principal's office, I was hit by the chilled air from the air-conditioning. Mr Prateek was already seated and going through some papers. The peon offered him a glass of water as I waited with bated breath. He drank water as if he had been thirsty for years. The peon uncle knew me well. His face was etched with worry as to why I was there. He gave me a look and walked out hurriedly.

The principal left me gulping with anxiety. I was still standing close to the door when he looked at me and said, "Come, sit."

I adjusted my collar and seated myself with some effort. I made as innocent a face I could to save me from some of the impending trouble. He put his paperwork aside and crossed his fingers.

"What's your name?" he asked with concern in his voice.

"I am Fauji, sir," I replied ardently.

"Fauji, I have never seen you here before, why?"

I replied with some thought, "Sir, I work in the garden, with my father."

"I inspect the garden every day, how come I have never seen you?"

I kept quiet. How could I tell him that my father had kept me from his sight? Why? I didn't know either.

Surprisingly, Mr Prateek seemed like an understanding person; he didn't insist and changed the subject. "So, you're the son of our gardener Hari?"

"Yes, Sir."

"Why do you toil in the garden? Don't you have school to attend?"

"Sir-sir, I-I…"

"Don't be scared. Just tell me." He offered me some water and I took it.

I hadn't realised till that point that I was extremely thirsty. I drank all the water and carefully placed the glass back on the coaster.

"Yes, Sir. I am his son."

"Do you know how to write? To read?"

"I do, Sir."

He nodded and offered me a diary. It seemed like his personal journal. I opened it and saw a quote written on the first page. Overwhelmed, I read it with broken confidence:

"If you want to shine like a sun, first burn like a sun, by A.P.J. Abdul Kalam."

At the end of the sentence, I remembered how I was burning just a few minutes ago, when I had run away from the school canteen. I, too, was burning.

Mr Prateek found me lost in my thoughts and asked, "So, you do know how to read. Let's see if you can do basic math." He offered me a sheet of multiple choice questions. I looked at it and felt confident. I knew how to solve all of them. He gave me a pen, noticing the glint in my eye, and timed me. I marked all the answers correctly, counting on my fingers. When I was done, I realised he had been looking at his watch.

"Mm, a little slower than average, but you have answered correctly."

I was feeling so giddy! I was liking how the day was turning out! I was enjoying this little session with Principal Sir. I think he understood that I was fond of studying. Feeling a sense of accomplishment, I sat in my chair respectfully.

"Sir! Principal Sir!" It was my father; he was calling out from outside. Peon Uncle came inside to ask for permission. "Sir, he is insisting—the gardener."

"Let him in."

I suspected if Peon Uncle had anything to do with informing my unassuming father, who must have been busy pulling out weeds from the field.

"I am very sorry for this, Sir. He won't do anything like this again. Fauji, say sorry to Sir," my father said and gave me a look. It was worse than the look my mother gives me when I refuse to eat vegetables.

"There's no need to say sorry. Hari, why don't you send him to school?"

My father was tongue-tied just like I had been. However, I was surprised when he expressed everything honestly. My father was truly a humble man. He said, "Sir, I want him to go to school, but I don't have the means to send him to a good one."

I looked at the principal, who was deep in thought. He said, "Do you know your son is a bright student?"

Surprised, my father looked at me and said, "I—You're very kind, Sir."

"Hari, would you like to work in the library? You could be the assistant to our librarian Miss Rita. She will help you figure everything out."

My father couldn't believe his ears. I think I even saw tears in his eyes. He folded his hands and said, "Sir, you have a big heart. You really do. How kind of you."

"However," Mr Prateek said sombrely, "I do have one condition."

"Anything, sir, anything."

"I want Fauji to take admission here in my school."

Our jaws dropped to the ground in shock. I could almost hear my mother jump in excitement. We couldn't believe that her dream for me was finally going to come true. My father came back to his senses and said, "Sir, this is so kind of you, I could never pay you back for this."

"I am doing my school a favour, Hari. If a student like Fauji studies here, I will be extremely proud." He then turned to me and said, "Would you like to join our school, Fauji? Will you study with all your heart and mind? Will you make your father proud?"

Of course, I loved to study! I had never imagined I would have access to the huge library, the spacious classrooms, the great playing field, the basketball court that glimmered under the golden sun, the students... Yes, I was going to be one of them now. Weird how life can take a 180-degree-turn in a few moments. The very place I was running from, was now standing before me with open arms, inviting me to become its part. With a glint of renewed hope in my eyes, I nodded and said, "Yes."

COMPUTER!?

While there's much to explore, I don't like going out into the world. I would rather stay at home and watch cricket. I feel at home with my friends, watching television with them and enjoying the fresh popcorn we roast at home. On the weekends we all go to work, and after coming back, we enjoy a movie or a match. My name is Chhotu—that's the name my folks have given me. I work at the nearby restaurant with my group of friends. We wash dishes and clean the floors. On weekends we do another job which is exclusive to my country India.

You know we have the seven days in a week; in English they call them Monday, Tuesday, etc. In Hindi they're called *Somvaar*, *Mangalvaaar*, *Budhvaar*, *Guruvaar*, *Shukravaar*, *Shanivaar*, and *Ravivaar*. While normal people enjoy the weekend, I and my friends go out on Saturdays to collect alms and mustard oil in a forsaken plastic container. This is especially done on Saturdays to please the Saturn God. People believe that donating coins and oil on a Saturday to the poor will bring them positivity and good health.

It's because of this belief that we confidently go out asking not just for alms and oil, but also for food, clothes, shoes, etc. The devout and generous never hesitate to give something on this day. Hence, we're sure to take some money and cooking oil back home. When the ration at home becomes scarce, we never shy away from asking for flour as well. This is the week plan of us ten to twelve year olds. While I am the oldest in my group, I always let my friends guide me. We exchange notes on which houses to visit, which block is the most generous, how to ask for the alms, and what to do if the gates shut on our faces.

I listen to them silently and gather all the information they have. Then, I make it clear for everyone by repeating the game plan. "First, you have to leave home at sharp 6 in the morning. Go to the temple first, you will find many devout people who are mostly generous there. Pray to Devi Maa and thank her for the alms we get at her doorstep. When done there, we will get breakfast. If anyone of us do not receive any donation, we will give a part of our earnings to him. After having our breakfast, we are to head to our blocks and go knocking door to door. We have to ring the bell several times, remember, because people already know it's us. Only a few come out at the first ring of the bell. We have to keep insisting and if needed, just call out, 'Aunty! Aunty!' They will soon get irritated and come out. Act extremely meek and innocent when they do come out and just extend your plastic container. We will meet for lunch when the sun is straight above our heads, and head back home. Okay? Understood?"

With this, our Saturdays start. We eagerly look forward to lunchtime, so we can count our earnings and grab lunch together.

I am familiar with the streets, each block and house—who lives there, what their temperament is. I know a few houses where they're even aware of my name. They give me good amounts of flour and oil, along with ten-rupee coins and something to eat. There is one house in particular where I always get fifteen rupees. I have to knock a few times, but a girl comes out eventually. She is much older than me, must be twenty-something. Every single time—it even makes me giggle a little—she opens the door with an irritated expression and complains about the incessant bell-ringing.

"I have told you many times, I can hear it the first time you ring. Have you gone crazy?"

"Sorry, Didi. I am very sorry. I won't do it again. Sorry, didi," I say.

She graciously shakes it off and pours some oil and a few coins into my container.

"Didi, don't you have anything to eat?"

She shakes her head again, a gesture of having forgotten all about it. Within a few minutes, she arrives with two chapatis wrapped in aluminium foil.

"Is it enough?" she asks.

I nod. That's how our interaction ends for the week.

However, that day, just as I am about to leave to get to another house, she stops me and asks, "What's your name?"

That's odd. She has never asked me anything before that day.

"Chhotu."

"Hmm, Chhotu, why don't you attend school?"

That is quite direct, but I tell her the real reason anyway. "Because I have to earn a living." My voice is urgent—my lunch is waiting. She, however, doesn't get the hint and asks me more questions.

"How old are you?"

What does it have to do with you? Leave me alone.

"Twelve, Didi," I reply with a meek voice.

"So, you're a twelve-year-old boy, and you don't go to school. Have you ever been to a school?"

My comrades will leave without me! Just stop poking your nose in my hustle!

"No, Didi, I have never been to a school."

"Oh, what?!" She is shocked as if I have committed a huge crime.

"Haan, Didi…"

"How long are you planning to do this?" she asks with command in her voice.

She doesn't think much, does she? I am going to do this for as long as I can. What's wrong with this?

"I don't know, Didi. I do this every Saturday."

"Haan, that I know, but are you going to do this all your life? What do you do on weekdays?"

I surrender; she is adamant at finding faults in my daily bread. "I work at a restaurant. I wash dishes there."

She shakes her head again. It seems with every detail I reveal, her disappointment just grows and grows. "So, are your parents okay with this? What do your father and mother do?"

Okay, now that gets me thinking for the first time. I decide to give in to this uncalled-for conversation.

"My father doesn't work. Mother died in childbirth."

"What? He does nothing? And you go out to make a living at this age of studying and playing?"

"Hmm."

"That's pathetic. You must tell him you want to study. If you do that, you'll be able to become someone respectable. Then you will be earning instead of begging, you hear me?"

"*Haan*, Didi." Completely clueless about how to dodge these balls coming at me one by one, I surrender and keep repeating the same thing with a losing heart. I don't think there's anything wrong in doing what I do. I get some time away from my abusive father who does nothing but drink his day away. I feel a great relief when I'm away from him. And moreover, I feel great for not having to rely on him for my expenses.

"You should think about this. Get your name enrolled in a government school. It doesn't take much."

"*Thik hai* (As you say), Didi," I say and continue on my way.

"You should understand. You cannot keep doing this forever. Become something more. Become someone better," she remarks and goes inside.

I don't know why, but nobody has ever thought of giving me advice before. Nobody has ever talked to me about the future. I have always been like a plastic bag, clueless and directionless in the flowing wind. But she has stopped me and stirred a storm of questions in my soul today.

I thought I wanted to join my friends for lunch, but now what I want more than anything is to go home and ask my father about my education. If not that, I can learn practical skills like basic English, MS Word, or computer typing. I know the cyber café-wale bhaiya has learnt the same, and now he doesn't have to go begging like before. He has been able to rent a small shop for himself. My mind is on fire—I want to leave begging. I can already see the shop in my mind. With great bold letters on a rectangular board, it would look like this:

CHHOTU CYBER CAFE
Print Outs, Photocopy, Passport-Size Photo

Having made up my mind already, I finish my biryani in one go and declare to my buddies, "I won't come to beg anymore."

It is met with some audible gasps, while some of them don't even bat an eyelid. They go on eating, expecting I will explain myself. I was hoping for a more dramatic reaction, however. To emphasise myself, I repeat, "So, I won't come to meet you on Saturdays anymore. *Thik hai? Tata!* (Ok? Bye!)"

Still no reaction. I wonder when they will become mature enough to think of more than just a plate of biryani—these kids! Only if they had an ounce of ambition like I do. Just as I am about to walk away, one of them pipes in, "*Oi!* Do you think you will be able to convince him?"

He means my drunkard father. Well, I'm surely going to let him know about my desire. He will nag and rebuke me right away, I know. And then, I will stay silent and keep doing what I'm supposed to do. He will express strong objection at my not bringing him the Saturday alms, but I know what I want to say. Seeing Didi's attitude today has given me some inkling of how I am supposed to live my life. She is just a girl like many others, but she doesn't act like them. She is different in the way she carries herself, in the way she stands with her arms crossed. She could be just another girl next door, but she isn't. She has inspired me to be something more that I had no problem being. She has jerked me out of a sleep. I do not want to go back to snoring anymore. I am going to try my luck with my father for sure. Whatever he says, I will make sure that I am the one thinking of my future, even if he isn't. I will take responsibility as much as I can. Whatever happens next, I will be ready for it too.

Hmm, who is this new person? I didn't have the slightest idea of who I could be with a little nudge of motivation.

With a spring in my step, I return home. As soon as the tin door of my little hut comes into view, I feel a fear creep up on me. My father's angry face flashes before my eyes, and I feel weak in the knees. I huff once, remember God, and step inside.

"Aye! What have you got today? Show me." As expected, my father caught the sound of my footsteps, even though I was being quite furtive.

Left with no choice, I walk up to him. I gulp my saliva and show him the plastic container that has the mustard oil and about twenty ten- and five-rupee coins. He looks thrilled upon seeing them. With a glint in his eyes, he rushes to the kitchen, pouring the oil into the old steel container. Then, he almost scratches the bottom of the container to retrieve the oil-soaked coins. He washes them with the running water of the community hand pump outside. With the sticky oil still coating the coins and his fingers, he counts them quickly.

"A hundred and fifty? Only?!" he exclaims. His sparkling eyes turn red and furious. He gives me a glare that chills my blood. I feel like I'm unable to speak. My senses leave me; my fingers go cold. I know what he is going to say next, I have heard it many times before.

"You! Did you steal?"

"No," I say. That is all I can manage to blurt out.

"Show me your pockets! Right now!" He gestures to me to come closer, and I amble forward with my head hung low. He furiously frisks my old cotton shirt and dusty short pants given to me by strangers, not him. I have known since my early years that my father will never get me anything—he won't celebrate my birthday; he won't even give me any fatherly advice.

With a loud groan, he pushes me back and scratches his head. "Why? Why are you slacking? Don't you have any duty towards this family?"

Something snaps inside my head. "Family?"

He is stupefied. He can't believe that I had talked back. I can see it in his eyes. But I have already made up my mind.

"Did you just talk back to me?"

"Father, I don't want to beg anymore. I will learn basic computer, like Harish Bhaiya."

"What? You, and computer!?" He bursts into a guffaw that our neighbours across the street must've heard. "Don't be a brat now! You're just a street dog, understood? Just like I was, you are my offspring, and so you are the same. Stop dreaming, rascal!"

But I have made up my mind. So I say, "No, father, it doesn't matter. What matters is what I am going to do now. I am going to learn basic computer, and then I will open a shop. I will not fund your alcohol anymore. You need to become a responsible father now." I don't even know how I was able to come up with so much courage. Somewhere inside my mind I can hear Didi smiling at me brightly. A part of me is overjoyed.

My father is speechless. He puts the coins in his hands on the floor and stands up from his old tattered bed where he used to spend all his hours. He doesn't look at me and silently trudges out of the hut. He has never done this before. Usually, with the coins, he always rushes to the beer shop to get his dose for the night, but today he just leaves it like it is nothing.

I pick them up and put them safely in my cupboard. They will help me pay the fees to learn computer typing for one day at least. For the rest, I have my savings from washing dishes.

INVISIBLE

"They're getting high," I tell the reporter of a channel I have never heard of before. They showed me they had about half a million subscribers on YouTube. I didn't mind the attention.

"What? With the glue?" the reporter asks me, baffled. She must not have the slightest idea. She looks that way for sure—naive, new at her job, not much older than me. She is dressed not much better than I am either. Pressed and washed, that's the only difference.

"Not just glue, they can get high on anything—glue, balm, nail polish remover, whitener pen, etc., you know?" I explain to her. Watching her expressions change from unpleasantly surprised to slightly disgusted to pity is interesting. She doesn't show it on camera, though—it is facing me. It is her micro-expressions she needs to work on if she wants to be a good reporter.

"It's really bizarre. Why do they do this though?" she follows up with a usual and logical query.

"To forget hunger," I reply, matter-of-factly. She noticeably winces this time. I add, "So many of us here don't get a complete meal. We rarely eat to our heart's content. I have been able to arrange for a better life for my four siblings and myself, but most of us in this area, we don't eat. It turns into an addiction before they know."

"So..." The reporter is at a loss for words. I see her searching for the right words to speak her thoughts, if there are any, given that she is affected by us slum kids, the invisible kids. At least she has made it here, or her channel has. Perhaps she is an intern. Doesn't matter, she is welcome, for the big channels never cover us.

On the television, they blabber about a lot in nice suits. Those issues seldom make sense to us. All they talk about are the powerful and the rich. They discuss them, cover them, and invite experts to fight on their behalf. We are invisible—we have always been—not a part of the society. And here she is, in her modest kurta and jeans, covering us. It did feel weird at first. I was worried if I should even speak to a channel I had never heard of. But then, what's the harm, I had thought.

"So, uh, has anyone ever come to visit you? NGOs, government organisations?"

"Yes, they come, but we like it here."

"What? Why?"

How do I answer that? Simply because we know all too well that they take money from people in our lieu but spend only a fraction on our welfare. We have trust issues. And mainly because we have a community here. We might be living in slums, but we network and help each other. We might not have a gas stove, but we cook together in the open.

"Because everyone is here," I say.

"Your community is here. That's why you don't leave."

"Yes, they come for the kids; they mostly want to support the kids, sometimes women, but what's the point?"

"They provide education, shelter, a nice place that is, and you get clean water, you can take a bath everyday—is it not good?" she replies, making some valid points.

"Yes, it is, but everyone gets education for the sake of making money. We have been making money since we're little, providing for ourselves. I don't see the point."

"The point is, you will be able to read and write. You will have access to the bigger world. You can become anything you want."

She does make sense, but how do I tell this to all the kids around me? They never listen; they're either busy getting high or they are out on the streets, picking rags and begging, or doing odd jobs.

"This is precisely what I try to do with my open lectures," I say, "I do want them to get a broader perspective on life."

"You have become quite famous in the local area—known as Lecturer Gudiya. How did you do it?"

That makes me look back to two years ago when I was a nobody. I still am, but at least my work has given me some name among the local press. I was only fourteen when I had gathered some money and decided to spend it on an entry-level smartphone. Everything I needed was going to be available on it. I had to keep the sum hidden from my family, but it's all worth it now.

"I wanted to study, read, and write. I knew free classes were available on YouTube. I didn't have the time to attend school, nor did I have a tutor available," I say.

"Oh, so you are self-taught! That's incredible!" She smiles at me in admiration.

"I learnt everything—Hindi, English, Math, and Science. It's very interesting. I still attend classes every day. Then, I decided it was not enough. I wanted everyone around me literate as well. That's how I decided to host open lectures on Sunday afternoons. I study each day in the evening. Going from one locality to another, I find kids who are wasting away their time smoking, getting high, or just playing around, and I ask them to learn from me for free. This one old bedsheet is all I carry other than my smartphone. I spread it under a shade and teach them for about an hour or two, sometimes more."

"This is great work you are doing. You're not only supporting yourself, but also helping other kids. How do people react to this?"

"When I teach, sometimes people, the young mostly, come and tell me I am doing great. They make videos of me and ask me to take a selfie with them."

"You are a celebrity now," she comments, offering me a chance to pause and smile. Little does she know what I am going to say next.

"Actually, sometimes, the police come and disperse my classes. I don't feel like a celebrity then."

"Oh, what do they say?"

"They don't say anything, they just come swinging their truncheons and shoo us away."

"How often does it happen?"

"Every now and then. I don't give up though." A smile spreads on my face unintentionally. I guess being a bit of a rebel is what I enjoy.

"What is your ultimate goal in life, Gudiya?"

"I want all of us, these kids, to be able to read and write. Because of people's encouragement, I have started my YouTube channel and Instagram page. I do want to become a real lecturer," I say and burst into a giggle.

"Really! How many followers do you have?"

"About 5,000 on Instagram and 10,000 on YouTube."

"Wow! Well done! It's really remarkable what you're doing, Gudiya. What message would you like to give to our viewers?"

"Come to my classes, if you can. And if you cannot come, watch me on YouTube and Instagram."

And then, with a huge smile on my face, the interview ends. The reporter shakes hands with me, takes pictures with me and my students, and drives away in her channel's car.

It was my first time getting interviewed, and I look around to find admiring eyes. My work has just gotten started. In a world that wants to keep us at bay, act like we don't exist, there will always be something to do. In the future, I am going to need more people to empower us—the invisible kids.

CENTRE OF GRAVITY

Born and brought up on the streets, I have stayed all my life inside tents that we install in each new village and city. We are in the show business, but we don't make as much as the Bollywood stars. We don't even attract as big a crowd. Even if we do, we remain anonymous. My family of four—mother, father, me, and younger sister—we make money by performing for the crowds on the streets of India.

Imagine the chaotic colours of a regular Indian street, the overstimulation of traffic honking, revving of engines, blaring of bullet bikes, calls of hawkers, random eighties and nineties songs, chiming of the little bells on bicycles—a lot going on in one moment. In this chaos, we look for a place to set up the stage for our show. Finding a peaceful spot is a challenge, but we manage by politely asking people for some space. First, we clean the spot and check the strength of the soil to see if it can hold our stage in place, the four poles set into the soil as a pair of Xs, about thirty feet from each other, or as much as the space allows for. Then, we set up the stage for our show, which is not a platform with props over it, but a path, a narrow path, probably even narrower than the choices life has given us.

My father brings out a coiled lump of rope, the one they make with jute and straws, uncomfortable for the hand to hold. He unwinds it and ties the rope tightly to one side. He winds it around the meeting point of the poles several times, his muscles glistening under the sun, and then he ties a secure knot with strength and agility. He walks with the other end of the rope and ties it to the other intersection of poles. He pushes the tied rope down to check if it is secured in the air, ten feet above the ground, and with that, the stage is ready for the show to begin.

The performer is my nine-year-old sister. She has been taught to walk the tightrope ever since she learnt to walk. She has broken her bones several times as well. Being the elder brother, I have volunteered multiple times to replace her, but my parents say the crowd will give more money if a girl performs.

So, I have no choice but to go around, collecting the day's earnings from the jaw-dropped, gaping-mouthed onlookers. My sister shows nothing on her face as she takes the balancing pole in her hand and walks ahead with a watchful step. With wobbly feet, she quickly gains her balance and makes a silent pact with the tight rope. My father's fixed gaze doesn't waver from her, and he stands guard to catch her if needed.

I watch my sister in awe as she makes her way on the fine line between disaster and applause, tense gazes and relief, and between winning the day's bread and sleeping with empty or partially-filled stomachs. In a grimy pink kurta and a beaten red salwar, my sister balances herself. People come and stop to watch her, gathering in numbers, and then someone says, "Selfish parents, using their kids for income." Then someone replies, "*Majboori, sahab, sab karva hi leti hai.* (Compulsion of circumstances, Sir, forces one to.)"

I feel relieved when the comment of the first gentleman does not disperse the crowd. I know my father is worried about the same when I glance at him. My sister has heard it as well, but she doesn't flinch. A roar of applause erupts, and I know my sister has made her way to the end.

Now it is time for her to turn around and walk back. The crowd has to be kept hooked for as long as we can. Carefully, she walks back, but her left foot suddenly jerks, and she goes to and fro like a pendulum. My father steps forward hastily, ready to catch her, but she knows her centre of gravity and quickly regains her composure. With a brief sigh, my father relaxes and grabs some water.

The show is a great success; we have made enough money to sustain ourselves for a few more days. But that is never going to be enough for us to have a proper shelter. We again spot a place to set up our tent for the next few days, as a fair is going on in this village. I think of taking my sister to the merry-go-round but hesitate to ask my father. As we wistfully stare at the children enjoying the various rides, mother comes over and quietly hands us twenty rupees. "Go! Before he finds out."

My sister giggles, I shush her, and then we head to the fair. This is our getaway, when we forget about everything. We just become kids, going wherever our hearts take us, guided by our eyes and propelled by our little running feet. We spot the merry-go-round that we want to ride and wait for the people to alight, so our line can get on. Holding my sister's hand, I trot up the narrow steps and sit inside the little octagonal open chamber with opposite seats. We peek outside through the rails and watch ourselves go higher and higher. Our stomachs tickle and we hold each other's hands tight. Suddenly and gradually, everything starts becoming smaller. We see people becoming ants, shops turning into boxes, trees changing to shrubs, and our little tent—*wait, where is it?*—is nowhere to be seen!

"Hey, do you see our home?" I ask her.

She has a sharp eye and immediately spots the tiny indigo dot on the outline of the fair. She points and exclaims, "There is Maa! She is there!"

"How did you even spot it?"

"We had cleaned the area around it, silly. That's how."

My sister, she is lost in the view, not afraid at all, of course. She is fond of heights ever since; she has no choice. And here I am, a little scared for her, lest she fall. Unconsciously, I have taken on the role of my father. As the ride goes round and round, we wish it would never end, and so we don't realise when it ends.

"More! More!" my sister insists on staying on the ride.

"That's all the money we have got, sister. Let's go home now," I tell her, smiling, careful not to let the smile and wonder fade away from her eyes. I extend my hand towards her and whisper, "You won't have to walk on a tightrope anymore, sister. I am going to find something better to do—something not as daunting. I am going to talk to father about this. And I will make sure you can take as many rides as you want."

DEVI

My village has been hit by a flood.

My two sisters and I have no other option but to walk miles, day and night, to the city to find food, shelter, and possibly employment. In our ragged and soaked clothes, we walk through any locality that come our way. People meet us with strange gazes, but we know it is just the beginning. Clad in sarees that have lost all their vibrant colours and turned dull, my sisters look older than they really are. They are fluent in English, and so am I. In our village, most of the folks speak in English.

We don't know Hindi. And in the city we have reached, there are only Hindi speakers. We go from door to door, knocking, ringing bells in order to get some food first. The rest can be figured out once we have had something to eat. Nobody opens their doors for us—perhaps they wonder why so many young women are walking in a group begging, when they could be working. But we don't give up. Finally, at the end of the colony, we find one home with a little garden outside. At the entrance, there is a picture of Maa Durga. I don't know why, but I have a feeling they are going to help us. When we knock, a girl in her early teens opens the door. She gazes at all of us with curiosity.

One of my sisters says to her, "*Shishter*, do you have any food?"

The girl hesitates, wondering if she should speak in English too, but then listens quietly and understands. She replies in English, "Uh, yes, but my parents aren't home yet."

"That's alright Shishter, we only want some food. We don't need money," my other sister adds.

She nods and goes inside quickly. She even leaves the door unattended and open—quite naive and yet so refreshing for us. We linger outside for a minute. Finally, she emerges with chapatis and some cooked vegetables and offers us a seat as well. Our hearts are moved by this gesture.

After giving all our thanks to God and blessings to the girl, we start eating and finish in a few seconds.

"Shishter, could you bring us some water?"

She fetches a large tumbler of water promptly, and with our stomachs full, we give her some more blessings. She looks at me and says, "Chhotu, why? Don't you go to school?"

My sister steps in and answers, "We will send him to school once we find some work. Our house was all ruined in the floods."

She listens with sympathy but stays silent. I am awestruck at her simplicity. She has no strange gaze, no questions, no doubts—only a warm hospitality her parents must have taught her. She nods, understanding our situation, and asks us to wait for a moment more. She goes inside and brings back a pile of books.

"These are my old books that I was going to sell to the *kabaadi-wallah* (scrap dealer) anyway. Please keep them. Perhaps they will help you while you're still looking for accommodation."

She hands those books to me along with some change. She doesn't know what a great help this is going to be in the time that will unfold next. Her generosity makes her stand taller than she actually is. I know I want to be someone like that. Not so naïve, probably—maybe she doesn't know the harsh realities of life yet, or maybe she does and chooses to be kind. In that moment, I feel great admiration and love bubble up inside me for her. I think she is my first crush. I want to tell her that my real name is Mohan, not Chhotu. However, having the guts isn't necessarily my thing. I am used to being spoken for by my sisters. But now at least I have something new emerging in my heart after a long time, as if a flower bud has sprung out of the cracks in concrete.

It's time to leave. I turn to depart with my sister, her hand on my shoulder. I look back. The girl smiles at me and waves goodbye, but I can't even smile back and shy away.

Soon, my sisters find a place to work as a maid and a cook. Within a month, they even rent out a place, and I continue with my studies because of the books. One day, my sister comes home with a box of laddoo and tells me that she is thinking of getting me admitted to a private school. I squeal in delight and she quickly adds, "But you have to clear this admission test first. Only then they will allow you. And what's more, they will reduce the fees by half if you score above 90%."

My smile drops slightly after hearing that, and I ask her, "Then why have you gotten me these sweets, Didi?"

"Because I'm quite sure you will ace the test."

"When is it?"

"Tomorrow."

Yeah, that's my Didi, she likes throwing surprises like that. I forget she is my sister, full of surprises. It's funny how once one's life becomes a little more comfortable because of an income, their true personality gets a chance to shine. This little gesture, bringing home a box of sweets, is an expression of her personality, enhanced by resources.

I remember how both of them used to wear faded, soiled sarees and roam from our village to the city in search of accommodation and income. Even though we are living in a little flat now, I can only imagine what else is awaiting us when we have a little bit more. Back in the village, we were impoverished. The flood was the one thing that had forced us to come to the city. The only hope my sisters had was for me to study and get a nice and respectable job. I too wanted that. It was heart-wrenching when our little hut was ruined in the floods. Everyone we knew was crying and pleading with God: "Why? Why? Why have you forsaken us?"

There was help available from the government, but for how long could we live on glucose biscuits and bread? We needed more than the packets that were being handed out to us as if we were cattle. Our humanity was at stake as long as we stayed there, waiting for them to bring us relief. So, collectively, our neighbours and we decided to move base.

It was a tough journey. We had little money, and anything that belonged to us had been snatched away by the flood. Whatever little we had, we wrapped inside a *potli* (packet) and left. Suddenly, we felt like beggars, walking barefoot and looking around to see where we could find something to eat. Even though we knew English, nobody would take us in even for a basic job because of the way we looked. We were not illiterate, just hit by God's wrath. My sisters often discussed why the world was the way it was. I listened to them and felt that complaining would get us nowhere. So, I initiated the idea to leave, instead of living on the alms of the government.

We all understood how unexpected life was in that one event. Everything we had was destroyed in seconds. In seconds! How long does it take for one to build something of value? Years! People toil for their whole lives, and they still don't have a house to their name. How fickle ours was. It swam away in the raging flood like a bunch of straws, which it was. I often think: what if our straw hut was never taken away by nature? What if we still lived there, content, because everyone else was doing the same? There was not much one could do in that place—cattle rearing, farming, washing dishes and doing *jhadu-pocha* (sweeping-mopping) in the houses of the affluent who were rich but illiterate. That's what we all had. If the flood hadn't taken our world by storm, we wouldn't have a clean field to start over.

Back to what I was saying. In the city, spoken English is considered a skill, so my sisters want to teach at a school when they have saved up enough to not live here anymore. Anyway, I ask my sisters what I should be studying for the test. They give me confused looks, admitting they have no idea either, and that I should refer to the books the girl has so generously given to us.

I do just that. My heart fills with worry and anxiety as I study more and more. Hallucinations of what could happen and all that had happened to us cloud my mind, scaring me to death. Every time I feel like putting the books away and snoozing for a minute or two, these nightmares wake me up. The screams of people who has lost everything, the ruined and flooded village, people drowning, pale white packets of glucose biscuits floating in the gushing water—I see and hear everything. With a jerk, I wake up, my heart beating wildly. I look around and see that everyone is okay. Nobody is drowning, no packets are floating, we have a roof over our heads—a concrete one—which shelters us from the harsh sun and the rain, which our old hut could not do. As there is no time to take a breath of relief, I decide to study everything I can from these books, no matter if it is in the test syllabus or not.

One thing I have understood very clearly is that in life, anything can happen at any moment, and storms are meant to take away everything that is making you idle and too comfortable to grow. This is the key learning that has taught me not to be happy with just this shelter we have right now, even though my sisters are enjoying this new place of stability. But I know there is more to us than this. I know what we can be, and it is no time to celebrate. We still have to go a long way before we can have a real life. What exactly is "life"? I don't know. Probably, it is the relentless pursuit of everything better, of becoming someone better, of making people's lives better—at least of the ones we love. But that girl, she had no relation to us. We were total strangers, beggars at her doorstep. But she opened up the gates of her house for us when nobody else did. She welcomed us without a question. She fed us and gave me the gift of knowledge through these books. She taught me the value of being selfless to those we don't know. Being good to those who have no relation to us whatsoever can be so rewarding for the other party that they might be able to dream of a new life altogether, like I was doing right now.

I decide that for her sake I must ace this test. And then, when I get admission, I would love to go to her house and thank her with all my heart. I don't know if she will remember me. But the image of Maa Durga outside her house symbolises the presence of a Devi in that dwelling. To me, she is that, Devi, the one who gives with all her heart, and that too with a smile. It fuels me all the more to drink up all the knowledge in these books.

As dawn breaks, my sister wakes me up with the most beautiful smile on her face and says, "We got new clothes for you. Get dressed, we are going to drop you off at the school. The test timings are 9 a.m. to 10 a.m."

I check my old wristwatch; I was asleep for three hours. Immediately, I jump up from the bed and get dressed. My sister gets me a nice poha-and-ginger-tea breakfast. It gives a boost to my senses, and we take the rickshaw to the school.

I feel my parents standing right behind my sisters when I look back at them on my way to the exam hall. We had only one torn and faded picture of them, which was taken away by the flood. But their faces are always adorned in our hearts, and now I can see them waving at me and blessing me with such hope in their faces. How amazing it is when someone has expectations from you—it means they think you're capable of fulfilling them. With this belief, I step inside.

I look around the exam hall to find the other kids wearing nice shoes, shirts, and jeans. They flaunt nice hairstyles as well. They look well off, and I, well, I look like myself. I have zero shame in the way I look, because it has been earned by the hard labour of my sisters. My shirt is new, simple, and pressed; my hair is well-oiled; my face and hands are daubed with cream. My shoes are the cheapest, bought from a thrift market. And I am proud of it. I adjust my collar and pray to God. I remember asking him about a month ago why he had taken away everything from us. But now, I ask for his blessings for the life that is awaiting me because he has taken away the old one. I bow my head slightly and start writing.

After one hour I come out of the exam hall and spot my sisters chatting and enjoying tea at the chai stall outside. I appear in front of them, and immediately they order one more cup. I sit down beside them and the chai-wallah asks, "How did your exam go, champion?"

I realise that anything can happen, no matter what, so I choose my words carefully. So, even though I am confident of my answers, I only say, "Dada, it was a tough one. I hadn't expected this much difficulty. Now everything lies in Shiva's hands."

"Oh, I see," he remarks and returns to pouring tea from cup to cup to give it a nice froth.

"Our results will be out tomorrow. We should head back home now, Didi," I tell my sisters.

The next day, while I'm sleeping soundly after being completely exhausted, my sister wakes me up again, though not as gently as yesterday.

"Wake up! Wake up!" It feels like an earthquake, and I get up a little furious.

"Why aren't you letting me sleep? Don't you know I was so exhausted yesterday because of all the studying I had to do the whole night?"

"Hey, be a little gentle with him, okay?" my elder sister tells her and smiles mysteriously while sipping her chai.

"Why are you smiling like that?" I ask, puckering my brows.

"You got in!" the other one exclaims.

"What?! I got admission! Wow!"

"Not just that, you got the highest score! When we went to see your results, your name was at the top of the list, brother. We felt so proud that we started telling everyone that our brother had topped the exam. We distributed sweets among the staff, the guard, the helpers, and the chai-wallah as well."

"And now, it's your turn to have it," says my elder sister as she hands me a 100-rupee-chocolate. It is the most expensive gift I have ever received, after the books that were given to me so generously by that girl.

I suddenly remember her and tell my sisters, "I must go back to thank her!"

"What? Who?"

"Did you cheat in the exam?"

"Oh no, no, you're getting me all wrong, Didi. I'm talking about the girl who gave me these books. She is the reason why I was able to study. Shouldn't we go back to thank her?"

They both exchange looks and say with a smile, "Okay, you should go and thank her, but make sure her parents don't think that you are irritating her or something. Okay?"

"Yes," I say, as I try to recollect the way to her house.

I knock at the door, looking wide-eyed at Durga Maa's picture above their door. Someone appears from inside. It is her. She looks out and instantly recognises me.

"Arre! Chhotu! You look different now." She opens the door and asks me if I need to eat.

"No, I just came to thank you," I say, giving her the chocolate.

"What? What is this for? Why are you giving me this? I did nothing but help you in your time of need."

"Because of your generous hospitality to us complete strangers, I will be able to go to a nice school. My sisters are working now, and we are hoping to see better days."

"I still don't understand," she wonders, looking at me for an explanation.

"Because you had given me your old books instead of selling them to the kabadi-wallah, I was able to study for the entrance exam."

"Oh, I see now. That's so great! I had no idea. You looked like someone who was willing to work hard, so I didn't think twice before giving those books. If you need more, just come back here and I will give you new ones when my year ends. I hope you have enough money to buy the books for your curriculum?"

"Oh, yes! They gave me a cut in the school fees because I topped the exam. So, my sisters will be able to manage everything nicely."

Hearing this, she steps forward, accepts the chocolate, and pats my back. My heart leaps; I feel something I have never felt before. Then she says, "You will go places. It's just the beginning. Just wait and watch."

ACKNOWLEDGEMENTS

This book began as a murmur in the heart, shaped by countless quiet moments spent observing and learning from those who move through our world silently—the chai boys, the helpers, the flower-sellers, the street performers, the boys and girls who shoulder more than their age should allow. To them, India's invisible hands and untold stories, I owe the soul of this book. Thank you for teaching me resilience, humility, and the meaning of grit in motion.

To my late parents, Ruby Prasad and Kaushal Kishore, whose quiet wisdom and unwavering integrity shaped the foundation of my life—thank you for instilling in me the belief that every human being matters and that no labour, however humble, is ever in vain. This book is an extension of those values you lived every day.

To my wife Tulika, whose love and strength holds our family together, and to our younger daughter Mriga, who is proudly carrying forward the family's commitment to creating meaningful opportunities for underrepresented, low-skilled workers. Your actions give life to the ideals in these pages.

And to my elder daughter, Tushita—this book would not exist in its present form without you. You carried its emotional weight, sharpened its language. From thoughtful editing and structural shaping, to soul-level questioning, to pushing me to dig deeper, you helped Chhotu find not just its form, but its truth so that these stories feel lived and heard. Chhotu carries your fingerprints on every page.

A heartfelt thank you to Kevin Missal, CEO of NuVoice Press, for believing in this story and giving Chhotu a platform that honours its message. And to Navya and the brilliant team at Hubhawks, whose dedication to socially impactful storytelling ensured the book reaches hearts, not just shelves—thank you for amplifying the quiet voices at the centre of this work.

And finally, to every "Chhotu" I've ever met, and to every reader who picks up this book not just with their eyes, but with their heart…thank you. May these stories unsettle you in the best way. May they make you look twice, ask gently, and remember deeply. And if, someday, you pause to ask a child his name, you will have already begun to change the story.

— Aseem Kumar

ABOUT THE AUTHOR

Aseem Kumar is a first-generation entrepreneur, philanthropist, and passionate storyteller whose life journey—from wearing Bata shoes on Ranchi's streets to building boardroom empires—mirrors the very themes of hope, grit, and transformation that shape his debut book *Chhotu.*

Raised in the industrial heart of Ranchi, Aseem's early life was marked by modest means and outsized dreams. He rose through the ranks with resilience and drive, eventually founding Kaurub Exports, a successful venture built from the ground up without financial backing or legacy advantage. Alongside his business success, Aseem has remained deeply rooted in social responsibility—his company is inclusive of disabled workers and committed to uplifting communities across Jharkhand, Delhi and NCR.

Chhotu is a reflection of his lived empathy, born not from theory but from a life spent observing and engaging with the children who serve, hustle, and vanish into the margins of Indian society. In giving them a voice, he also gives them dignity. His philanthropic work, passion for equality, and keen understanding of India's socio-economic divides breathe life into each character.

Outside of his professional pursuits, Aseem is a fashion model, adventure motorcyclist, and gourmet chef—proving that reinvention knows no age. His life and work are grounded in one unshakable belief: that every underdog has a story worth telling—and worth hearing.